CABINETRY BASICS

Sam Allen

Sterling Publishing Co., Inc.   New York

Metric Equivalents

MM—MILLIMETRES   CM—CENTIMETRES

INCHES TO MILLIMETRES AND CENTIMETRES

INCHES	MM	CM	INCHES	CM	INCHES	CM
⅛	3	0.3	9	22.9	30	76.2
¼	6	0.6	10	25.4	31	78.7
⅜	10	1.0	11	27.9	32	81.3
½	13	1.3	12	30.5	33	83.8
⅝	16	1.6	13	33.0	34	86.4
¾	19	1.9	14	35.6	35	88.9
⅞	22	2.2	15	38.1	36	91.4
1	25	2.5	16	40.6	37	94.0
1¼	32	3.2	17	43.2	38	96.5
1½	38	3.8	18	45.7	39	99.1
1¾	44	4.4	19	48.3	40	101.6
2	51	5.1	20	50.8	41	104.1
2½	64	6.4	21	53.3	42	106.7
3	76	7.6	22	55.9	43	109.2
3½	89	8.9	23	58.4	44	111.8
4	102	10.2	24	61.0	45	114.3
4½	114	11.4	25	63.5	46	116.8
5	127	12.7	26	66.0	47	119.4
6	152	15.2	27	68.6	48	121.9
7	178	17.8	28	71.1	49	124.5
8	203	20.3	29	73.7	50	127.0

Library of Congress Cataloging-in-Publication Data

Allen, Sam.
  Basics : cabinetry / by Sam Allen.
    p.   cm.
  Includes index.
  ISBN 0-8069-8290-X (paper)
  1. Cabinet-work.   I. Title.
TT197.A44   1991
684.1′6—dc20   91-12939
                                                    CIP

10 9 8 7 6 5 4 3 2

© 1991 by Sam Allen
Published by Sterling Publishing Company, Inc.
387 Park Avenue South, New York, N.Y. 10016
Distributed in Canada by Sterling Publishing
% Canadian Manda Group, P.O. Box 920, Station U
Toronto, Ontario, Canada M8Z 5P9
Distributed in Great Britain and Europe by Cassell PLC
Villiers House, 41/47 Strand, London WC2N 5JE, England
Distributed in Australia by Capricorn Ltd.
P.O. Box 665, Lane Cove, NSW 2066
Manufactured in the United States of America
All rights reserved

Sterling ISBN 0-8069-8290-X   Paper

Series editor: Michael Cea
Edited by Keith L. Schiffman

Basics Series

Band Saw Basics	Scroll Saw Basics
Radial Arm Saw Basics	Sharpening Basics
Router Basics	Table Saw Basics

Other Books by Sam Allen

Making Cabinets & Built-Ins
Making Kitchen Cabinet Accessories
Remodelling & Repairing Kitchen Cabinets
Wood Finisher's Handbook
Wood Joiner's Handbook

CONTENTS

INTRODUCTION

This book is intended for beginners. It provides all the basic information and step-by-step directions first-time cabinetmakers need to build cabinets. If you follow the instructions carefully, you'll soon be able to make many types of professional-looking cabinets (Illus. I-1 and I-2).

As you will learn, cabinetmaking can be a productive and easy-to-learn craft. The materials used for the cabinets described here are available at most lumberyards and home supply centers. The cabinets are designed so that you can build them using a few basic tools and one simple joint—the dowel joint. Many professional cabinetmakers use the dowel joint in their highest-quality cabinets (Illus. I-3).

This book is divided into eight chapters. The first chapter covers basic information you'll need before you can begin to build—the tools and materials that will be used, and the proper safety procedures. Chapter 2 gives a visual and descriptive overview of the system of cabinetmaking presented in this book. This system, the "frameless," or the "32 mm" system is the most up-to-date method of cabinetmaking. This versatile

Illus. I-1. *If you follow the directions carefully, you'll be able to build cabinets that look professionally made. These modular freestanding cabinets are described in chapter 6.*

Illus. I-2. *Built-in kitchen cabinets are described in chapter 7.*

Illus. I-3. *The dowel joint is very versatile—it can be used to make virtually any type of cabinet you want. This dowel joint is the same type that many professional cabinetmakers use in their highest-quality cabinets.*

system is most closely associated with the sleek lines of European built-in cabinets, but it can be adapted to traditional styles and to freestanding cabinets (Illus. I-4, I-5, I-6). Chapter 2 also

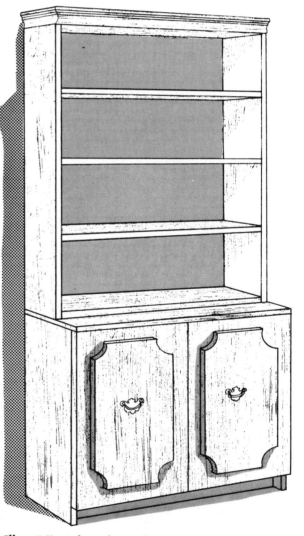

Illus. I-4. *You'll learn the most up-to-date system of cabinetmaking, the "frameless" system or the "32 mm" system of cabinetry. This versatile system is associated with the sleek lines of European-made cabinets, like the one shown here.*

Illus. I-5. *A frameless cabinet can be given a more traditional look with the addition of a cornice, and some moulding on the doors.*

shows how to build the basic box (the "carcass") of the cabinet.

Chapters 3 and 4 show how to build doors and drawers, with many design variations. Chapter 5 describes finishing methods, including directions for applying veneer tape to the edges of both plywood and particleboard, applying stain and varnish to lumber or plywood, and painting particleboard.

Freestanding cabinets are described in chapter 6. Step-by-step directions cover the construction of two types of modules that can be combined in various ways to make different cabinets.

Chapter 7 describes built-in cabinets, and shows how to build both base cabinets and overhead cabinets.

Chapter 8 gives directions for applying plastic laminate to cabinets.

With the information presented in this book, even the most inexperienced woodworker will find himself building high-quality cabinets.

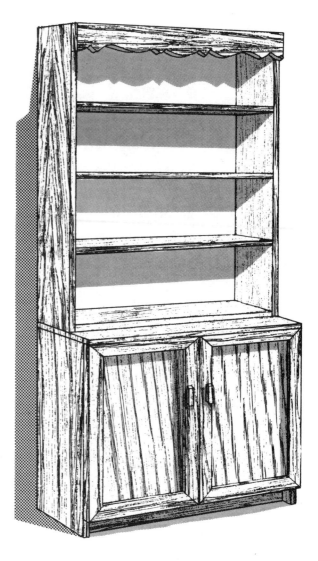

Illus. I-6. *Adding some "gingerbread" to the top, and adding a different style of moulding to the doors gives this cabinet an Early-American look.*

1

MATERIALS AND SAFETY TIPS

Before you learn about the cabinetmaking process, be aware of the tools and materials that are necessary, and how to use them safely. These aspects are discussed below.

Tools

Since this book is meant for the novice cabinetmaker, I've kept the number of tools to a minimum (Illus. 1-1). To build cabinets using the system in this book, you must have the following tools and supplies:

safety glasses or goggles
dust mask
hearing protectors
hammer

tape measure
(with both English and metric scale)
square
2 C clamps
4 bar clamps
portable electric circular saw
portable electric drill
drill jig with bits and drill stops

A dowelling jig is very important—it's used to make all of the joints. There are several types of jigs available. Be sure to buy a jig that will position holes in both the edge and the face of a board. Some types will only position the holes in the edge of the board, and they won't work when used for cabinetmaking (Illus. 1-2). Several companies make dowelling jigs that work well. The jig I use (as shown in the photos in this book) is the Arco No. 582. Other jigs may require a slightly different setup, but they'll follow the same basic directions. Follow the instructions

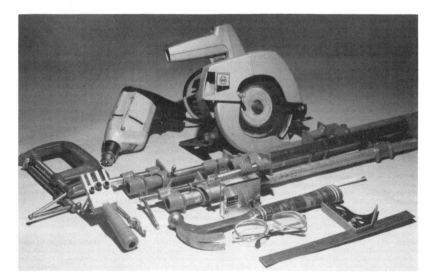

Illus. 1-1. *Since this book is meant for the beginner, the number of tools necessary has been kept to a minimum. This photo shows all of the tools necessary to build the basic cabinets shown in this book. Pictured here: C clamps, a dowelling jig, a portable electric drill, a portable electric circular saw, bar clamps, a tape measure, a hammer, safety glasses, drill bits, and a steel square.*

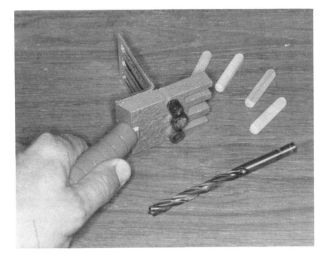

Illus. 1-2. *The dowelling jig is very important—it's used to make all of the joints. There are several types of jigs available. Buy one that positions holes in both the edge and the face of a board.*

that come with your jig. Some other jigs that can be used to make edge joints are: Disston Dowel Magic, Wolfcraft Dowel-Master, and Record No. 148.

In addition to the tools listed above, several other tools make the work easier, but they're not absolutely necessary. These include: an electric sander, a block plane, a sabre saw, and a backsaw (Illus. 1-3). A couple of sawhorses also come in handy.

Safety

Cabinetmaking can be fun and safe if you observe the proper safety precautions. Always read and follow the directions that come with your tools. Wear safety glasses when you saw, drill, or do anything that produces flying chips or dust. Hearing protectors keep loud machinery from damaging your hearing. A dust mask keeps wood dust out of your lungs.

As you work, keep your fingers away from the cutting edge of tools. If you have long hair, tie it back. Don't wear loose clothing (neckties or oversize sleeves, etc.) because if it catches in the drill bit or the saw blade, it will pull you into the machine. Remove your rings and other jewelry, because they can also get caught in machinery.

Be alert when you work. Don't work if you're tired or sleepy. Never work when you're under the influence of drugs or alcohol.

Materials

The materials discussed in this book are all readily available at lumberyards and home supply centers. You can use the techniques described with ¾"-thick lumber, plywood or particleboard. Each is described below.

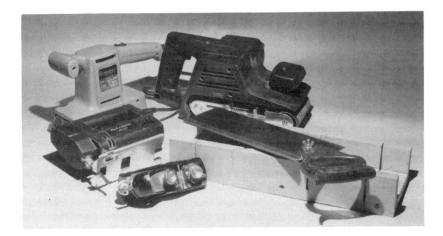

Illus. 1-3. *The tools shown in this photo will make it easier to build the cabinets, and they allow you to add decoration to the basic cabinet. Pictured here: two types of electric sander, a sabre saw, a block plane, a backsaw, and a mitre box.*

Illus. 1-4. *Lumber can warp and cup, making it difficult to assemble cabinets.*

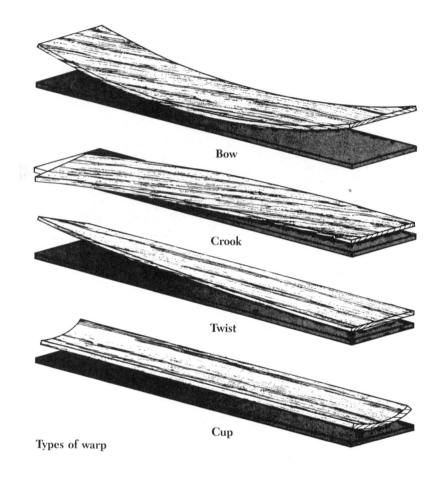

Bow

Crook

Twist

Cup

Types of warp

Lumber

Lumber has several advantages as a cabinetmaking material. First, it's already cut to width, so you don't need to make long cuts with the saw. Second, it is easy to add a finish to. Third, since it is solid wood, the edges will take a finish as well as the face does.

The main disadvantage of lumber is that it warps and cups, making it difficult to assemble the cabinet (Illus. 1-4). Careful selection of the lumber that you buy can minimize problems with warping and cupping. As you select the lumber, examine it closely. The edges should be straight and the face should be flat, not cupped. Knots and other surface defects aren't as important a consideration as warping and cupping, because you can lay out the parts to minimize most

serious defects. Allow about 20 percent extra material when you buy lumber, so that you can cut out the defects.

Pine is the most common type of lumber available. Pine works well for cabinetmaking, and it can be given a variety of finishes.

Hardwoods such as Philippine mahogany, oak, alder, and maple are available at some large lumberyards (Illus. 1-5). These woods are all more expensive than pine, but they are more durable and they give a different "look" when given a finish.

Lumber sold at most lumberyards has been surfaced on all four sides. For cabinetmaking, you need lumber that is ¾″ thick. It is called 1″-thick lumber, although it's actually only ¾″

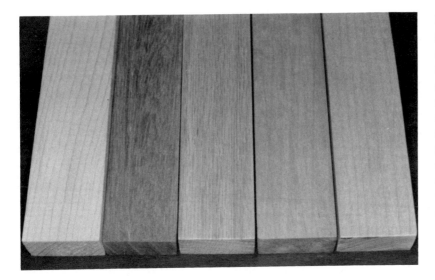

Illus. 1-5. *Pine (far left) is the most common type of lumber available. Pine works well for cabinetmaking, and it can be given a variety of finishes. Some hardwoods are available at large lumberyards. Shown left to right (after the pine strip) are: Philippine mahogany, oak, alder and maple. These hardwoods are more expensive than pine, but they're more durable and they each have a different "look" when finished.*

thick. Lumber comes in several standard widths; the width is also rounded off to an even number, so that the actual width will be slightly less than what the board is called.

The sizes of lumber used most often in these projects are 1 × 4 ("one by four"), 1 × 6, 1 × 8, 1 × 10, and 1 × 12. Lumber is usually available in 8′, 10′, 12′, and 16′ lengths. Choose a length that will allow for the most efficient layout when you cut out the parts.

Plywood

Plywood is made of several thin layers ("plies") of wood that are sandwiched together (Illus. 1-6). Plywood comes in sheets that are 4′ wide and 8′ long. Common plywood thicknesses are: ¼″, ½″ and ¾″. Plywood's main advantage is its stability; it won't warp or cup under most normal conditions. Its main disadvantage is that its exposed edges are difficult to finish. Chapter 5 describes how to apply wood-veneer tape to hide the plies.

You'll have to make long, straight cuts to cut out the cabinet parts from a sheet of plywood. Chapter 2 explains how to use a board as a guide to do this.

Fir is the most common type of plywood. It can be stained and varnished, but when the appearance of the material is very important, you may want to use plywood that has a hardwood face

veneer. Hardwood plywood is expensive, but you can achieve a very beautiful finish.

Large lumberyards usually carry birch, Philippine mahogany, and oak plywood. Other types of plywood are available on special order.

Particleboard

Particleboard is a good material for the novice to use because it is versatile and inexpensive. Therefore, it would not be a tragedy if you were to make mistakes when working with it.

Particleboard is composed of small particles of wood that are glued together under pressure (Illus. 1-6). Particleboard comes in 4′ × 8′ sheets and in several thicknesses. The boards shown in this book are ½″ and ¾″ thick. Particleboard is stable (like plywood), so cupping and warping are not problems.

Since there is no grain pattern on the face of particleboard, it is almost always painted or covered with plastic laminate. Special procedures are needed to achieve a smooth paint job on particleboard, and, like plywood, the edges must be covered before a finish can be added. See chapter 5 for details and techniques for achieving a smooth finish on particleboard. When covered with plastic laminate, a particleboard cabinet can be durable and attractive. Particleboard makes a very good substrate for plastic laminate. Chap-

Illus 1-6. *Plywood is made of several thin layers ("plies") of wood that are sandwiched together. Plywood sheets are 4' wide and 8' long. Common plywood thicknesses are ¼", ½", and ¾". Particleboard is made of small wood particles that are glued together under high pressure. Particleboard comes in 4' × 8' sheets and in several thicknesses: The sheets pictured in this book are ½" and ¾". Particleboard is stable (like plywood), so cupping and warping are not problems. Particleboard is inexpensive. Since there is no grain pattern on its face, particleboard is almost always painted.*

ter 8 gives directions for covering cabinets with plastic laminate.

Hardboard

Hardboard (used for cabinet backs and drawer bottoms) is made from wood fibres that are pressed into thin sheets (Illus. 1-7). The projects in this book use standard ⅛"-thick hardboard. Hardboard comes in 4' × 8' sheets.

Plastic Laminate

Plastic laminate, a hard plastic material that's either ⅙" or ¹⁄₃₂" thick, comes in sheets that are 4' × 8', 4' × 10' or 4' × 12'. Many lumberyards and home supply centers also sell smaller precut pieces of plastic laminate. Many colors and patterns are available—wood-grain patterns are a favorite choice of many cabinetmakers, but solid colors and other patterns can also be used with

Illus. 1-7. *Hardboard (used for cabinet backs and for drawer bottoms) is made from wood fibres that are pressed into thin sheets. The projects in this book use ⅛″-thick hardboard. Hardboard comes in 4′ × 8′ sheets.*

dramatic results. Plastic laminate is durable and water-resistant, so it's a good choice for kitchen cabinets or for other cabinets that will be put to hard use.

Other Supplies

You should buy some additional supplies to assemble the cabinet (Illus. 1-8). Dowels and glue are needed for any cabinet you make. Buy aliphatic resin glue (woodworking glue). You'll need fluted dowels that are either ¼″ or ⁵⁄₁₆″ in diameter. See chapter 2 for more details on dowels.

If you make a cabinet with doors, you'll need hinges and handles (see chapter 3). Cabinets with adjustable shelves need shelf-support clips (see chapter 2). If the cabinet will have drawers, you'll need drawer guides (see chapter 4).

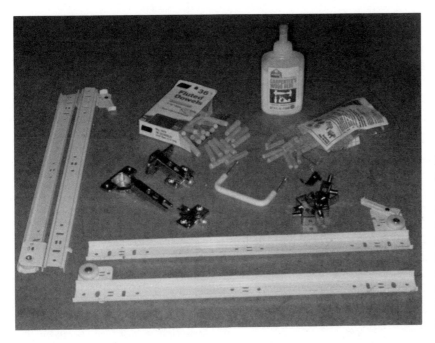

Illus. 1-8. *You'll need to buy some additional supplies to assemble your cabinets. Dowels and carpenter's glue are needed for any cabinet you make. If you make a cabinet with doors, you'll need hinges and handles. Cabinets with adjustable shelves need shelf support clips. If the cabinet has drawers, you'll need drawer guides.*

2
FRAMELESS CABINETRY

In "traditional" cabinet construction, a face frame is used on the front of the cabinet to strengthen the cabinet and provide a mounting surface for the door and the drawer hardware (Illus. 2-1). In frameless cabinetry, the face frame is eliminated, making construction simpler (Illus. 2-2). The functions of the face frame are assumed by the sides of the cabinet, with the addition of some special hardware. Since there's no face frame to strengthen the cabinet, a very strong type of joinery is needed to attach the cabinet components. Although nails, staples, screws, or special fasteners can be used in frameless construction, dowel joints are preferred (Illus. 2-3).

Frameless construction first became popular in Europe, where it's used to make built-in cabinets. The frameless system was introduced in the United States a few years ago, and it's gained in popularity ever since. Professional cabinetmakers often refer to it as the 32-mm system, because the hardware originally developed in Europe is designed for holes that are spaced 32 mm apart (Illus. 2-4).

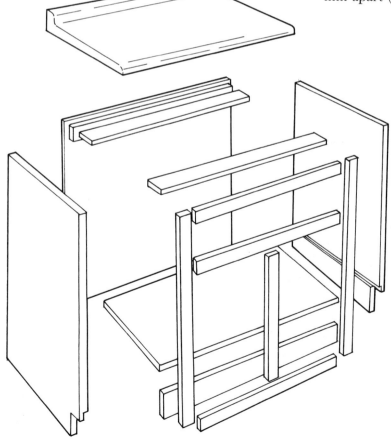

Illus. 2-1. *Traditional cabinet construction uses a face frame on the front for strength and to provide a mounting surface for the door and the drawer hardware.*

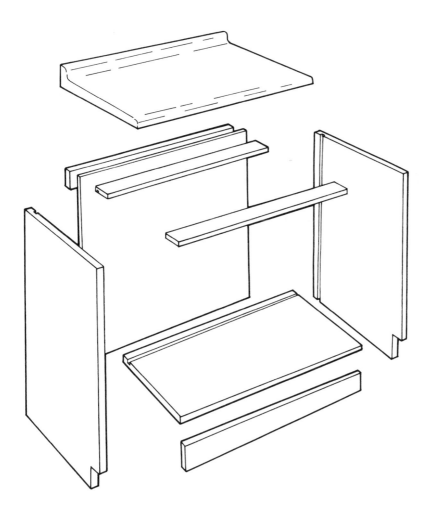

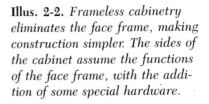

Illus. 2-2. *Frameless cabinetry eliminates the face frame, making construction simpler. The sides of the cabinet assume the functions of the face frame, with the addition of some special hardware.*

Illus. 2-3. *Dowel joints are preferred for use with frameless cabinetry. They're strong, easy to make, and they hold the parts in alignment during assembly.*

There are seven basic steps to making a cabinet using the frameless system.

1. Cutting the parts to size
2. Making a groove for the back
3. Making the dowel joints
4. Making the adjustable-shelf holes
5. Assembling the parts
6. Adding the doors
7. Building drawers

In this chapter, steps 1 through 5 are described. The other two steps are covered in chapters 3 and 4. After completing the first five steps, you'll have the basic box of the cabinet. Cabinetmakers call this box the *"carcass."*

In this chapter, I show how to make a very simple carcass. Later chapters will show you how to modify the basic carcass to make either free-standing cabinets or built-in cabinets.

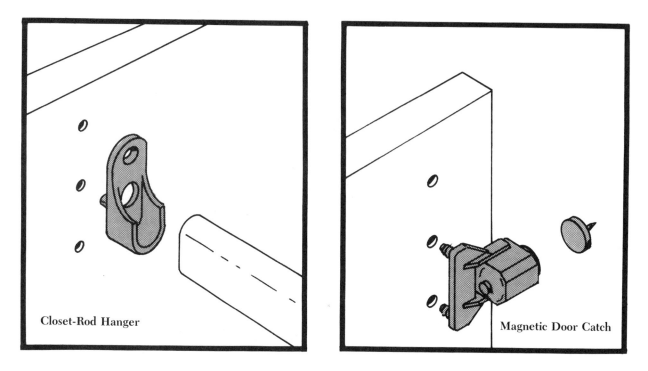

Closet-Rod Hanger

Magnetic Door Catch

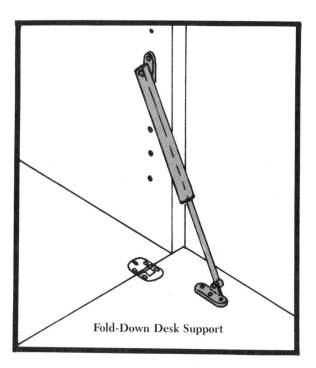

Fold-Down Desk Support

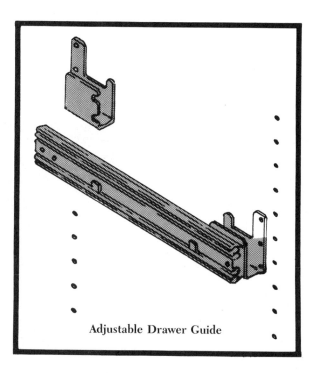

Adjustable Drawer Guide

Illus. 2-4. *Special hardware is designed to fit into holes spaced at 32 mm intervals. The four examples shown here are: a closet rod hanger, a magnetic door catch, a fold-down desk support, and an adjustable drawer guide.*

Cutting the Parts to Size

Begin by laying out the parts on the board (Illus. 2-5). Look at the plans to get the sizes of each part. The plans shown (Illus. 2-6, 2-7, 2-8) give the sizes used for a base cabinet with shelves.

If you use plywood or particleboard, cut the parts from a large sheet. First lay out the parts on paper. Arrange the parts to get the most efficient use of the sheet. It's difficult to stop a cut in the middle of the sheet, so lay out the cuts so that you can cut from one edge all the way across to the other edge (Illus. 2-9).

Now, mark the layout on the sheet. The factory edges of the sheet are straight and square, so use them as references. Always measure from a factory edge.

To make the lines parallel with a factory edge, make a mark at each end of the line, measuring from a factory edge. Then use a straight board or a yardstick as a guide, and draw a line between the two marks. Remember to include ⅛" between parts to allow for the blade width (Illus. 2-10).

Illus. 2-5. *Begin by laying out the parts on the board. Make a layout on paper first, then transfer the layout to the wood. Arrange the parts to use most of the sheet. It's hard to stop a cut in the middle of a sheet, so lay out the cuts so that you can cut from one edge all the way across to the other edge. Factory edges of the sheet are straight and square, so use them as references. Measure everything from a factory edge. To make lines parallel with a factory edge, make a mark at each end of a line, measuring from a factory edge, then use a straight board as a guide and draw a line between the two marks. Remember to allow ⅛" between parts to allow for the width of the saw blade.*

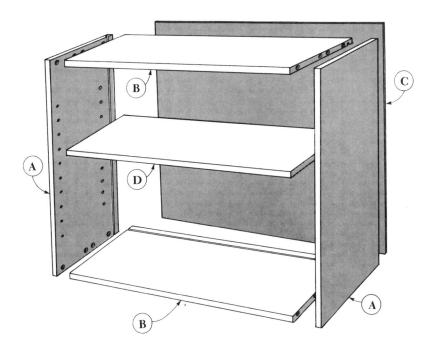

Illus. 2-6. *These are plans for the simple "carcass" to be built in this chapter. The parts are labelled: A (sides); B (top and bottom); C (back); D (shelf).*

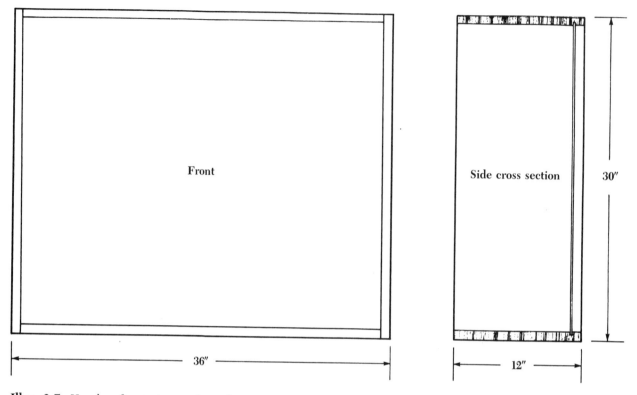

Illus. 2-7. *Here's a front view and a side cross section of the cabinet to be built in this chapter.*

If you use lumber, buy a board that's already cut to the correct width, and then lay out the length of each part on the board. Arrange the parts so that any defect falls in the waste area between two parts. Measure the length and make a pencil mark, then place the square against the edge of the board and line up the blade with the mark. Draw a line across the board using the square as a guide (Illus. 2-11). When you measure the next part, be sure to leave at least ⅛" between the two parts, allowing for the width of the saw blade.

Put on safety glasses before you cut. An experienced woodworker can often follow the line without a guide, but the novice should use a board to guide the saw. The cuts must be straight or the joints won't fit together well.

Measure the distance between the edge of the saw blade and the edge of the saw base. This measurement will be used to position the guide board (Illus. 2-12).

Next, position the guide board. The guide board should have a perfectly straight edge. The factory edge on a sheet of plywood or particleboard makes a good guide board. Use the measurement you got from the saw base to offset the guide board from the cutting line. Make sure that the saw kerf (the ⅛" cut made by the saw) will be on the waste side of the line. Make two marks, one near each end of the cut, and then line up the guide board with the marks. Use C clamps to attach the guide board to the work. Place the handle of the clamp down so it won't interfere with the saw (Illus. 2-13, 2-14).

If you tack a scrap of wood to the top of your sawhorses, you can place the sawhorses so that they support both sides of the cut. The saw blade will cut into the scrap, but it won't damage the sawhorse. The scrap wood can be replaced when it gets too ragged (Illus. 2-15).

Place the saw with the front of the base resting on the work, and the edge of the base against the

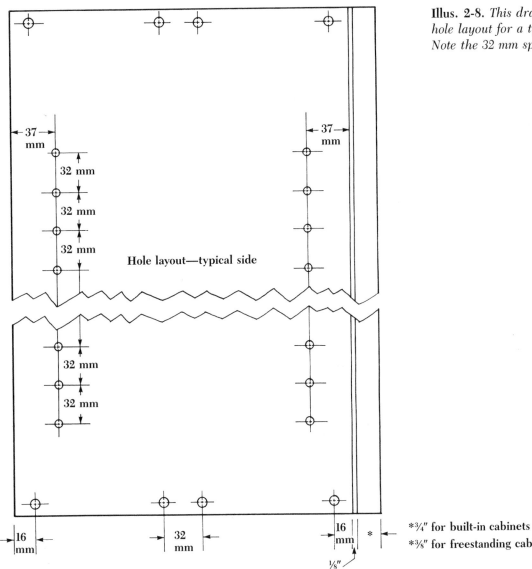

Illus. 2-8. *This drawing shows the hole layout for a typical side. Note the 32 mm spacing.*

37 mm

37 mm

32 mm

32 mm

32 mm

Hole layout—typical side

32 mm

32 mm

16 mm

32 mm

16 mm

*

1/8″

*3/4″ for built-in cabinets
*3/8″ for freestanding cabinets

Illus. 2-9. *First lay out the parts on paper to get the most out of one 4′ × 8′ sheet. This is the layout used for the carcass in the step-by-step photos. All of the parts were cut from half of the sheet.*

Make these cuts first.

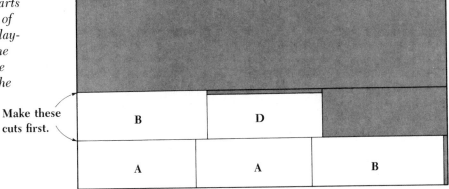

Illus. 2-10. *Measure everything for the layout beginning from a factory-cut edge. Make two marks near each end of the line, then use a straightedge to draw a line connecting the two marks.*

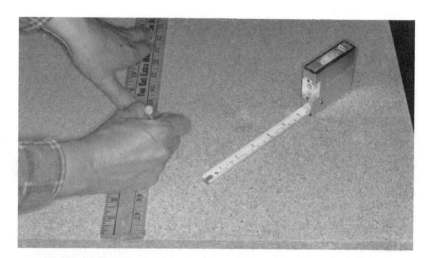

Illus. 2-11. *Place a square against a factory-cut edge to mark the cuts on lumber. Try to plan the layout so that defects like the knot on this board will be in the waste area, between the parts.*

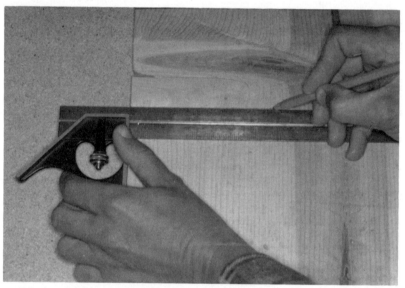

Illus. 2-12. *To use a guide board with a portable circular saw, you must know the distance from the blade to the edge of the saw base. Measure from the far side of the blade to the edge of the saw base. This measurement is used to offset the guide board from the cutting line.*

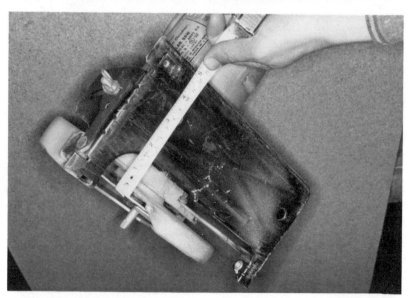

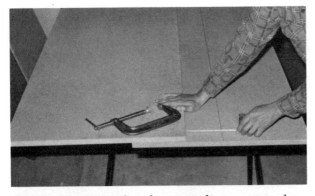

Illus. 2-13. *Now you're almost ready to cut out the parts using a portable circular saw. Set up a guide board to make the first cut. Use the measurement you got from the saw base to offset the guide board from the cutting line. The saw kerf (the ⅛" cut made by the saw) should be on the waste side of the line. Make two marks, one near each end of the cut, then line up the guide board with the marks. Use C clamps to attach the guide board to the work. Place the clamp handle down, so it won't interfere with the saw.*

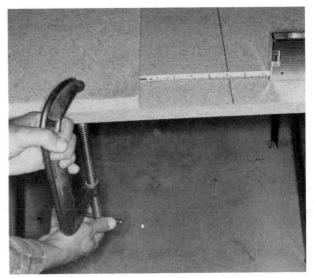

Illus. 2-14. *Place the guide board on the waste side of the line. Use the measurement you took from the saw base to offset the guide board from the cutting line. Clamp the guide board in place with C clamps.*

Illus. 2-15. *Attach a piece of wood scrap to the top of a sawhorse to allow you to cut across the sawhorse without damaging it. In this photo, the other part of the board being cut has been removed to show the sawhorse.*

guide board. The saw blade shouldn't touch the work. Start the saw and advance the blade into the work. Just as the saw starts to cut, stop it, and back it out. Check to see that the cut is just touching the layout line and that the kerf is on the waste side. If the cut is correct, then restart the saw and continue with the cut. Keep the base rubbing against the guide board (Illus. 2-16, 2-17).

Making a Groove for the Back

The ⅛" hardboard back fits into grooves cut in the sides, the top, and the bottom of the carcass (Illus. 2-18). Since a typical saw blade leaves an

Illus. 2-16. *Place the saw with the front of the base resting on the work and the edge of the base against the guide board. The blade shouldn't touch the work. Start the saw and advance the blade into the work. Just as the saw starts to cut, stop it and back out. Check to see that the cut just touches the layout line, and that the kerf is on the waste side. If the cut is correct, then start the saw again and make the full cut. The saw base should rub against the guide board.*

Illus. 2-17. *Make the first cut through the full length of the board, then cut the individual parts to length. Clamp a short guide board to the work and make the rest of the cuts the same way you did for the first cut.*

⅛" kerf, use the saw blade to make the groove for the back.

Unplug the saw and adjust the blade depth so that ⅜" of the blade is exposed below the base. Now, clamp a guide board to one of the parts. Position the guide board so that the groove will be ¾" in from the back edge of a built-in cabinet,

or ⅜" in from the edge of a freestanding cabinet. Make the cut, keeping the saw base against the guide board. This should produce a groove that's ⅛" wide and ⅜" deep along the full length of the part. Repeat this procedure on the other three parts.

Illus. 2-18. *Now make the groove for the back. Unplug the saw and adjust the blade depth so that ⅜" of the blade is exposed below the base. Clamp a guide board to the part. Position the guide board so that the groove will be ¾" in from the back edge of a built-in cabinet or ⅜" in from the edge of a freestanding cabinet. Make the cut, keeping the saw base against the guide board. This procedure should produce a groove that is ⅛" wide and ⅜" deep along the full length of the part. Repeat this procedure on the other three parts.*

Making the Dowel Joints

The sides, the top, and the bottom of the cabinet are joined together with dowel joints. To make these joints, get a good dowelling jig that you can place on the edge and the face of the boards (Illus. 2-19). A dowelling jig that only attaches to the edge of the board won't work!

You'll need two drill bits to go with the dowelling jig. One ¼" bit and one ⁵⁄₁₆" bit. A "brad-point" bit works best; it has a small point in the center that prevents the bit from wandering as you drill.

A depth stop is also needed for each drill bit. This is a small collar that fits around the bit. A setscrew holds the stop in place on the bit. The depth stop can be adjusted to control the depth of the hole made by the bit when you use the dowelling jig.

You'll also need dowels that have been specially prepared for the job. The dowels (available at most lumberyards, hardware stores, or home supply centers) have been cut to length, the ends are chamfered, and the sides are fluted (grooved). Fluting allows glue to be distributed evenly as the dowel is inserted in the hole, thus giving the dowel more holding power.

When making joints in ¾"-thick boards, use the ⁵⁄₁₆" bit. Use the ¼" bit when joining thinner boards. Professional cabinetmakers use a boring machine that drills all of the holes at once; the drill bits are spaced at multiples of 32 mm. Since you're drilling each hole individually, you could vary from this standard spacing. Since 32 mm is the industry standard, I use it in the following instructions.

Begin by laying out the dowel joint (Illus. 2-20). Place the two boards together as they'll fit in the finished cabinet. Make an X near the front edge of each board. Draw an arrow pointing to the outside of the cabinet on each board. Number each joint so that there won't be any confusion when it's time to assemble the cabinet.

For boards up to 12" wide, use four dowels. Wider boards require more dowels. If you use the type of dowelling jig shown in the photos, you'll mark only the dowel locations on both ends of either the top or the bottom board.

The first board will be used as a guide for the other boards. Make a mark 16 mm in from the front edge (Illus. 2-21). Find the middle of the board and make the mark. Now, make two marks, one on each side of the centerline, spaced 16 mm from the line. Now there are two dowel locations in the middle of the board. The dowels will be spaced 32 mm on center. A single dowel is placed 16 mm in from the groove at the rear.

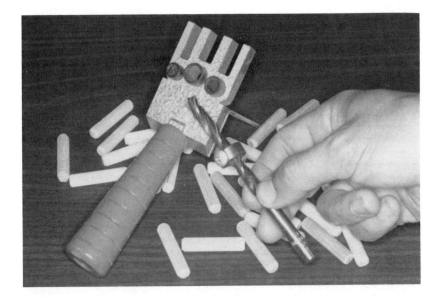

Illus. 2-19. *To drill the holes for the dowel joints, you'll need a good dowelling jig. You'll also need a depth stop for the drill bit. The dowels used have flutes (grooves) and chamfered ends.*

Illus. 2-20. *The following photos give step-by-step directions for making a typical corner joint using ¾"-thick boards. When making joints in ¾"-thick boards, use the ⁵⁄₁₆" bit. Use the ¼" bit when joining thinner boards. Place the two boards together the way they should fit in the finished cabinet. Mark an "X" near the front edge of each board. Draw an arrow pointing to the outside of the cabinet on each board. Number each joint so there won't be any confusion when it's time to assemble the cabinet.*

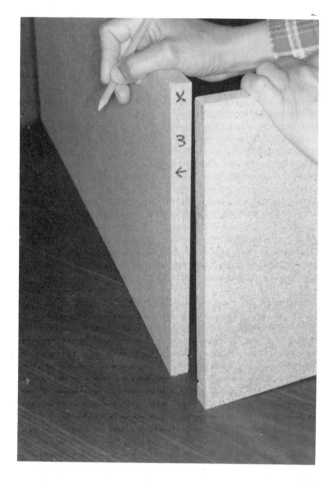

For boards wider than 12", start with a single dowel located 16 mm from the front edge. Measure 160 mm to the next dowel, and then 32 mm to the next. The next set of dowels is placed 160 mm from the previous location. Keep up this pattern until you get within 160 mm of the back edge, and then place a single dowel 16 mm in from the rear groove.

Illus. 2-21. *Lay out the dowel positions. Clamp the board to a sawhorse (end-up) while you mark the dowel locations and drill the holes. For boards up to 12" wide, use four dowels. Wider boards require more dowels. Make a mark 16 mm in from the front edge. Find the middle of the board and make a mark. Now make two marks, one on each side of the middle line, spaced 16 mm from the middle. This gives you two dowel locations in the middle of the board. The dowels will be spaced 32 mm on center. One single dowel is placed 16 mm in from the groove at the rear.*

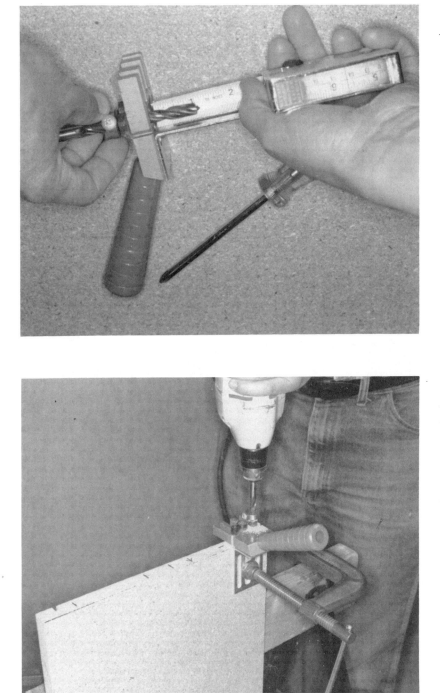

Illus. 2-22. *Prepare to drill the first set of holes. Place a depth stop on the drill bit and adjust the stop so that 1⅛" of the bit extends past the bottom of the dowelling jig when the depth stop hits the jig.*

Illus. 2-23. *Position the dowelling jig over the spot you've marked for the location of the first hole. Note the arrow that you drew indicating the outside face of the board. Place the jig so that the guide fence is against the outside face, and clamp the jig in place. Drill into the end of the board until the depth stop hits the jig. Remove the drill bit from the jig and reposition the dowelling jig over the next hole location. Drill the next hole, and continue in this manner until all of the holes are drilled. Now drill the holes in the other end of the board.*

Prepare to drill the first set of holes in the top (Part B) (Illus. 2-22). Place a depth stop on the drill bit and adjust the stop so that 1⅛" of the bit extend past the bottom of the dowelling jig when the depth stop hits the jig.

Position the dowelling jig over the first hole location (Illus. 2-23). The arrow that you drew shows the outside face of the board. Place the dowelling jig so that the guide fence is against this outside face, and then clamp it in place.

Illus. 2-24. *Temporarily place dowels in the holes you just drilled. Don't use any glue at this stage. These dowels will guide the jig when drilling the holes in the next board. Clamp the board with the dowels against the next board to be drilled. Align the boards so that the "X" is at the same end on both boards. Orient the arrows on both boards in the same direction. Place the jig's guide slot over the first dowel and clamp the dowelling jig in place with the guide fence against the outside face of the new board. Drill the hole, and then move on to the next hole location.*

Illus. 2-25. *Next drill the holes in the sides of the boards. Place a depth stop on the drill bit and adjust it so that ½" of the drill bit extends past the bottom of the jig. Use the previously drilled joint that has the same number written on it to guide the dowelling jig. Temporarily place dowels in the holes. Place the board to be drilled on top of the one with the dowels in it. Line up the board so that the "X"s are on the same end and the inside face of the side is on top. Line up the edges so that they're flush, and then clamp the boards together.*

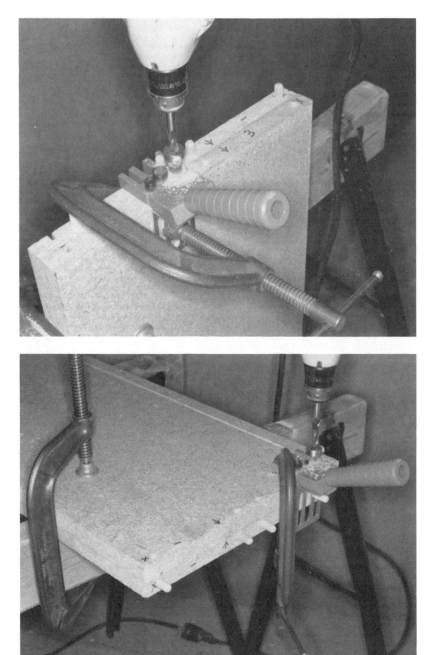

Drill into the end of the board until the depth stop hits the dowelling jig. Remove the drill bit from the dowelling jig and reposition the dowelling jig over the next hole location.

Drill the next hole, and continue until all of the holes are drilled, then flip the board end-for-end and drill the next set of holes.

Temporarily place dowels in the holes you just drilled; don't use any glue at this stage (Illus. 2-24). These dowels guide the dowelling jig when you drill the holes in the bottom (Part B).

Clamp the board with the dowels to the next board to be drilled. Align the boards so that the X (indicating the front) is at the same end on both boards. Orient the arrows on both boards in the same direction. The outside face of the board to be drilled should face out.

Place the guide slot on the dowelling jig over

the first dowel. Now clamp the dowelling jig in place with the guide fence against the outside face of the board to be drilled. Drill the hole, and then move on to the next location. Turn both boards end-for-end and repeat the procedure to drill the holes in the opposite end of the bottom (Part B). If you build several identical cabinets at once, use the first top (Part B) as a guide for the holes in the rest of the Part Bs.

Next, drill the holes in the sides. Place a depth stop on the drill bit with ½" of the drill bit extending past the bottom of the dowelling jig. Use the previously drilled joint (that has the same number written on it) to guide the dowelling jig. Temporarily place dowels in the holes.

Place the board to be drilled on top of the one with the dowels in it. Line up the boards so that the X's are on the same end, and the inside face of the side is on top. Line up the edges so that they're flush, and then clamp the boards together (Illus. 2-25).

Clamp the dowelling jig in a position aligned with the first dowel location. The guide slot in the dowelling-jig fence fits over the dowel below the jig. Drill down until the depth stop hits the

Illus. 2-26. *The shelves are held up by small clips that fit into holes drilled in the side of the carcass. The shelf height can be adjusted simply by moving the clip to a new hole, either up or down.*

dowelling jig. Remove the bit from the dowelling jig and reposition the jig to the next location. Continue until all of the holes have been drilled. Drill the rest of the joints; match the numbers on the guide board with the numbers on the board being drilled. Using the mating boards to guide the dowelling jig compensates for any errors in the dowel placement.

Making the Adjustable-Shelf Holes

The cabinet's shelves are adjustable. Rows of holes drilled in the sides of the cabinet accept small clips that support the shelf (Illus 2-26). You can buy these clips at most hardware stores or home supply centers.

A drilling guide makes drilling the shelf holes faster than if you measure each shelf hole individually. Make the guide from a piece of 2 × 4 lumber (Illus. 2-27). Get a straight piece that's reasonably free of defects. Cut a 24" length from the 2 × 4. Write TOP on one end and OUT on one edge, measure in 37 mm from that edge, and draw a straight line parallel with the edge. Next, make a mark every 32 mm along the line starting from the end marked TOP. The dowelling jig is used to drill a ¼" hole at each one of the marks.

Remove the guide fence from the dowelling jig and temporarily nail a board to the 2 × 4 to guide the dowelling jig. To position this guide board, line up the hole in the dowelling jig with the first mark on the 2 × 4. Make a mark on the 2 × 4 at the end of the dowelling jig. Do the same at the last hole. Line up the edge of a scrap board with these marks and attach it with a few nails.

Now, drill the holes in the 2 × 4 (Illus. 2-28 and 2-29). To line up the jig with the marks, put the drill bit in the jig and hold the jig so that it's slightly above the board. Press the point of the wood at the layout mark, and then slide the jig

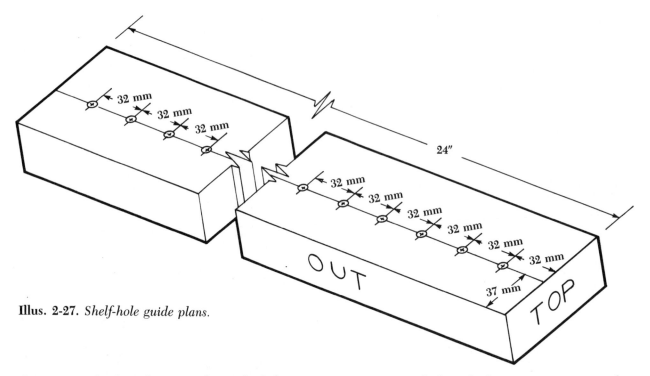

Illus. 2-27. *Shelf-hole guide plans.*

down onto the board. Press the end of the jig against the guide board that you nailed to the 2 × 4, and then clamp the dowelling jig to the 2 × 4. Drill all the way through the 2 × 4, and then repeat the procedure for the next hole. When all of the holes are drilled, remove the temporary guide board; the 2 × 4 is now ready to use as a guide for drilling the shelf-clip holes.

Now, use the 2 × 4 jig to drill the holes in the sides. If the sides are 24″ long (or shorter), align the end of the jig marked TOP with the top edge of the board. When the side is longer than 24″,

Illus 2-28. *Drill the holes in the guide accurately—the accuracy of all of the shelf holes depends on this jig. Use the dowelling jig to guide the bit. To position the jig, put the drill bit in the jig with the point of the bit extending past the bottom of the jig. Press the point of the bit into the wood at the marked location, then slide the jig down onto the board. Clamp the jig in place using a "C" clamp, then drill the hole.*

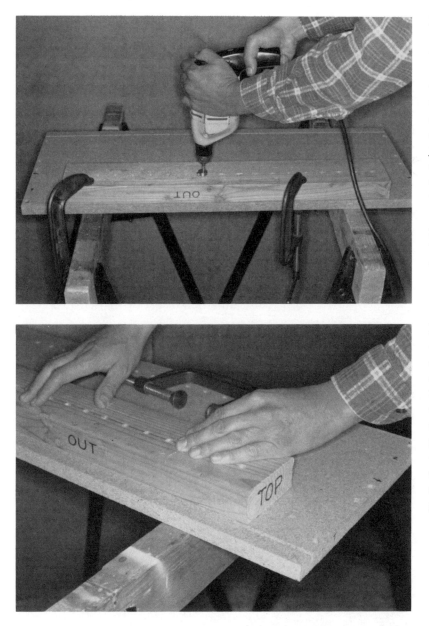

Illus. 2-29. *Now use the 2 × 4 jig to drill the holes in the sides. If the sides are 24″ or less in length, then align the end of the jig marked "TOP" with the top edge of the board. When the side is longer than 24″, divide the difference in half and measure down from the top of the side and make a mark to align the jig. Align the edge of the jig marked "OUT" with the front edge of the board. Use C clamps to hold the jig in position. Set the depth stop on the ¼″ drill bit to make a ½″-deep hole.*

Illus. 2-30. *Reposition the jig to drill the holes at the rear of the side. Turn the jig over so that the side that was against the face of the board is now up. Align the end marked "TOP" with the top of the side, or with the mark that you made for the beginning of the row of holes. The side of the jig marked "OUT" should now be aligned with the edge of the groove.*

divide the difference in half and measure down from the top of the side and make a mark to align the jig.

Align the edge of the jig marked OUT with the front edge of the board. Use C clamps to hold the jig in position. Set the depth stop on the ¼″ drill bit to make a ½″-deep hole. Place the bit in the first hole in the jig and drill until the depth stop hits the jig; move on to the next hole, and then continue until you reach the end.

Reposition the jig to drill the holes at the rear of the side (Illus. 2-30). Turn the jig over so that the side that was against the face of the board now faces up. Align the end marked TOP with the top of the side or with the mark that you made for the beginning of the row of holes. The side of the jig marked OUT should be aligned with the edge of the groove that the back will fit into. Drill holes in both sides. The cabinet is now ready for assembly.

Assembly

The back should slip into the groove easily. Test the fit before you begin assembly. If the fit is too tight, bevel the rear edge with coarse sandpaper wrapped around a scrap of wood (Illus. 2-31). If you have a block plane, use it to bevel the back—it's faster than using a sandpaper block.

Place one side (outside face down) on a solid working surface. Run a bead of glue along the joint, letting the glue drip into the dowel holes (Illus. 2-32). Let the holes fill up with glue about one third of the way. Don't let the hole get too full of glue, or the dowels won't go all the way in.

Spread the glue around inside the holes, using a sliver of wood (Illus. 2-33). This is very impor-

tant when you use particleboard, because when there's a large amount of glue left at the bottom of the hole, a chip can be forced out of the end of the board by the pressure generated by driving the dowels into the holes.

Put dowels in all the holes, and drive them all the way in, using a hammer (Illus. 2-34). Apply a bead of glue to the edge of the mating board (Illus. 2-35). Drip glue into the dowel holes until they're about one-third full. Use a sliver of wood to spread the glue around inside the holes.

Now place the mating board onto the dowels in the side (Illus. 2-36). Drive the joint tight by placing a scrap of wood on the other end of the board and hitting the scrap with a hammer.

Put some glue in the groove for the back on both boards and then insert the back (Illus. 2-37).

Illus. 2-31. *The back must slip into the groove. If it won't, bevel the back of the hardboard with a piece of coarse sandpaper wrapped around a small block of wood. It's usually necessary only to remove the fuzz left by the saw to get the back to slide into the groove.*

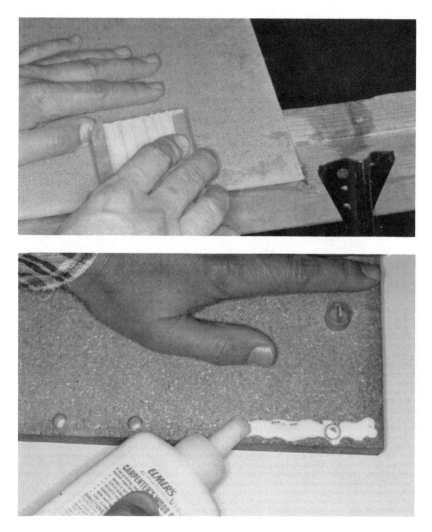

Illus. 2-32. *Run a bead of glue along the first joint, letting it drip into the dowel holes. Let the glue fill the holes about ⅓ of the way. Don't let the hole get too full of glue, or it will be hard to get the dowels to go all the way in. Use a sliver of wood to spread the glue around inside the holes.*

Illus. 2-33. *After you drip some glue into the dowel holes, spread the glue around inside the hole using a sliver of wood. If you leave a lot of glue at the bottom of the hole, you might split the boards as you drive in the dowels. Be particularly careful with holes in particleboard drilled near the ends.*

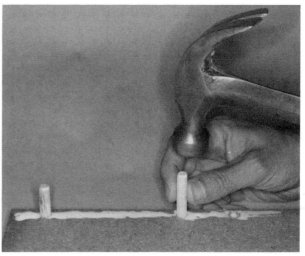

Illus. 2-34. *Put a dowel in each hole, and use a hammer to drive the dowels all the way in.*

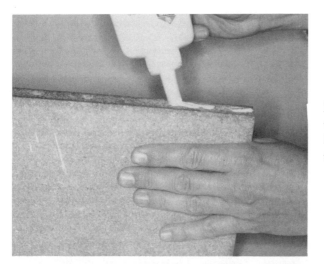

Illus. 2-35. *Apply a bead of glue to the edge of the mating board. Let the glue drip into the dowel holes until they're about ⅓ full. Use a sliver of wood to spread the glue around inside the holes.*

Illus. 2-36. *Now place the mating board on top of the dowels in the side. Drive the joints tight by placing a scrap of wood on top of the board and beating it with a hammer.*

Illus. 2-37. *Put some glue in the groove (for the back) on both boards and then insert the back. Repeat the procedure for the next joint. Apply glue to the groove for the back before assembling.*

Illus. 2-38. *The last two joints must be assembled simultaneously. Apply glue to both joints on the side and insert the dowels. Apply glue to the mating boards and the groove for the back. Place the side on top of the partially assembled carcass. Get all of the dowels started in the holes and make sure that the back is aligned with the groove.*

Repeat the same procedure for the next joint. Place the cabinet on its side and attach the other side. Before assembling, apply glue to the groove for the back.

The last two joints must be assembled simultaneously (Illus. 2-38). Apply glue to both joints on the side, and then insert the dowels. Apply glue to the mating boards and to the groove for the back. Place the side on top of the partially assembled carcass. Get all of the dowels started in the holes, and make sure that the back is aligned with the groove. Drive the joints tight, using a hammer and a scrap of wood.

Turn the assembled carcass face down and check it for squareness (Illus. 2-39), by measur-

ing the diagonals between the opposite corners. If the carcass is square, both measurements will be equal. If they're different, exert pressure on the longer diagonal until both diagonals are equal. You may be able to use hand pressure; if you can't, place a bar clamp across the diagonal from corner to corner and tighten it until the measurements are equal.

Clamp the joints tight, using bar clamps (Illus. 2-40). Remove any glue that squeezes out of the joints, using a dry rag. If you plan on staining the wood, try not to spread the glue around, because the glue will make a lighter-colored spot in the finish. Let the glue dry for at least one hour before removing the clamps.

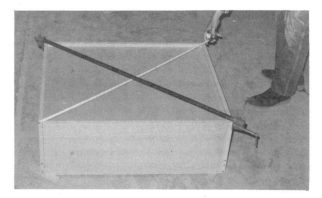

Illus. 2-39. *Turn the assembled carcass face-down and check the squareness by measuring the diagonals between opposite corners. If the carcass is square, both measurements will be equal.*

Illus. 2-40. *Clamp the joints tight using bar clamps. Use a rag to remove any glue that squeezes out of the joints. Let the glue dry for at least one hour before removing the clamps.*

DOORS

In frameless cabinetry, the doors constitute a main design feature (Illus. 3-1). They give the cabinet a modern look, or a traditional look, depending on the type of doors you choose. The door used for the cabinet shown in Illus. 3-2 is a full overlay door. The door completely hides the front of the carcass. Special hinges are needed, because the "normal" hinge attaches to a face frame. Hinges used with frameless cabinetry must attach to the *side* of the cabinet. Some hinges have adjustment screws that allow you to adjust the door after it's installed.

In this chapter, you'll learn how to make and install a simple type of door. Later in the chapter, you'll see how to modify a basic door to make different styles.

Constructing a Basic Door

Begin door construction by measuring the carcass to find the size of the door (Illus. 3-3). Measure from the outside of one side of the carcass to the outside of the other, and then measure from the outside of the top of the carcass to the outside of the bottom. Do you want to use a single door, or two doors? If you decide on two doors, divide the side-to-side measurement in half and subtract 1/16″ to determine the width of each door.

Cut the doors from particleboard or plywood (Illus. 3-4). Use a guide board, as described in chapter 2. Lay out the doors on the sheet, using factory-cut edges as measuring points. Use the offset measurement for your saw to position the guide board. Clamp the guide board in place, and then make the cut.

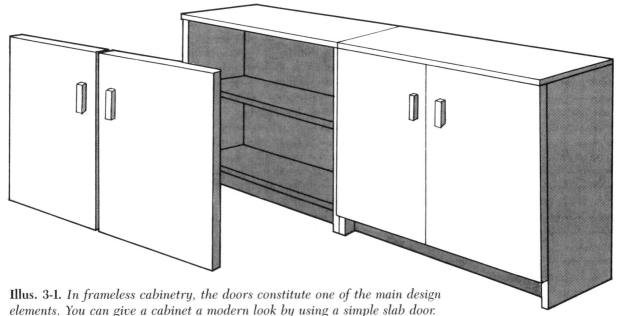

Illus. 3-1. *In frameless cabinetry, the doors constitute one of the main design elements. You can give a cabinet a modern look by using a simple slab door.*

Illus. 3-2. *Adding some moulding to the door gives a cabinet a traditional look.*

Next, install the hinges (Illus. 3-5). The hinge used for the door in this section needs a large hole in the back of the door (Illus. 3-6). For most uses, the measurement from the edge of the door to the middle of the hole is 2½″.

Buy a special drill bit, designed to drill hinge holes (Illus. 3-7). This special bit may be hard to find and expensive, so if you only install a few hinges, use a 1⅜″ spade bit that's been modified slightly (Illus. 3-8). The standard spade bit has a

Illus. 3-3. *Begin by measuring the carcass to find the size of the door. Measure from the outside of one side to the outside of the other, then measure from the outside of the top to the outside of the bottom. Decide whether you want to use a one single door or two half-doors. If you decide on two doors, divide the side-to-side measurement in half and subtract ¹⁄₁₆″; this formula will give you the width of each door.*

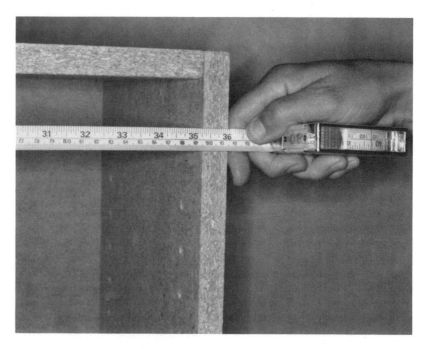

Illus. 3-4. *Cut the doors from particleboard or plywood. Use a guide board as described in chapter 2.*

Illus. 3-5. *Next, install the hinges. The type of hinge shown in Illus. 3-6 below needs a 35-mm hole in the back of the door. For most uses, the measurement from the edge of the door to the center of the hole is 2½". Use a special drill bit or a modified spade bit. Put some tape on the bit to indicate the depth of the hole. Stop drilling when the tape touches the surface of the door.*

Illus. 3-6. *A full overlay door completely hides the front of the carcass. Special hinges are needed, because hinges used with frameless cabinetry must attach to the side of the cabinet. The hinge shown here mounts in a 35 mm-diameter hole drilled into the back of the door. A separate mounting plate attaches to the side of the cabinet. The hinge slides onto the mounting plate and is locked in place with a set screw.*

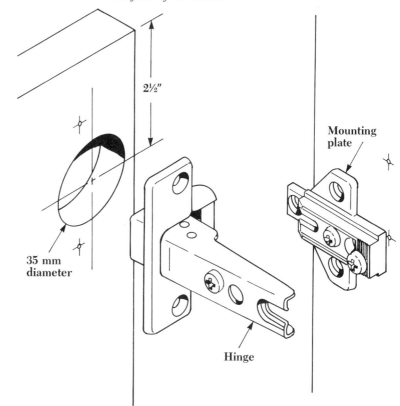

Illus. 3-7. *A special drill bit can be used to drill the 35 mm hole that you'll use to mount the hinge in the door.*

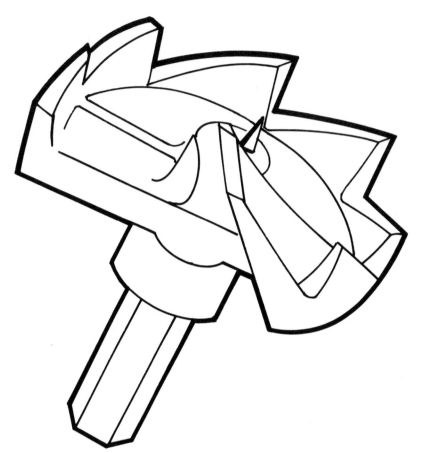

Illus. 3-8. *You can modify an inexpensive spade bit to drill the hole for the hinge. Use a 1⅜"-diameter bit. Grind down the spur so it won't break through the face of the door. The bit on the right has been modified for this purpose—notice that the spur is shorter than the one on the standard bit to the left.*

Illus. 3-9. *A small grinding wheel mounted in an electric drill can be used to grind down the spur. Clamp the drill to a table. Wear safety glasses as you grind. Follow the original spur angle and grind until the spur is about ¼" long.*

Illus. 3-10. *Drill a pilot hole for the screws that will attach the hinge. The pilot hole should be slightly smaller than the screw. Be careful not to drill through to the face of the door. Attach some tape to the drill bit to serve as a depth stop. Stop drilling as soon as the tape touches the face of the board.*

Illus. 3-11. *Install the hinge on the door. Place the cup in the hole, and then drive the screws into the pilot holes.*

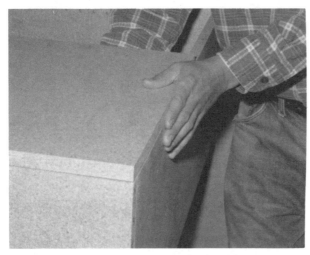

Illus. 3-12. *Temporarily attach the hinge-mounting plate to the hinge. Hold the door in position and mark the location of the mounting holes on the side of the cabinet. On a two-door cabinet, like the one shown here, lay the cabinet on its back and place the door on top in its proper position, then reach in from the other side to mark the hinge locations. When the cabinet has only one door, you will need to hold the door partially open to mark the hinge locations on the side.*

spur that's too long for this use; the spur would break through the face of the door before you could drill the hole deep enough.

To modify the bit, mount a small grinding wheel in the chuck of your portable electric drill. Clamp the drill to a table, and put on your safety glasses before you start to grind. Grind the spur of the spade bit (Illus. 3-9), following the original angle. Keep grinding until the spur is about $\frac{1}{4}''$ long. If the steel begins to turn blue as you grind, it's getting too hot. Stop grinding and cool the bit in a cup of water, and then start grinding again.

Mark the locations for the hinge holes on the back of the doors. Wrap masking tape around the drill bit to indicate the depth of the hole. Put the modified drill bit into the drill chuck, and then place the point of the spur on the mark. Drill down until the tape touches the surface of the board.

Drill pilot holes for the screws that attach the hinge (Illus. 3-10). The holes should be slightly

Illus. 3-13. *Drill pilot holes for the screws, then attach the hinge-mounting plate to the side.*

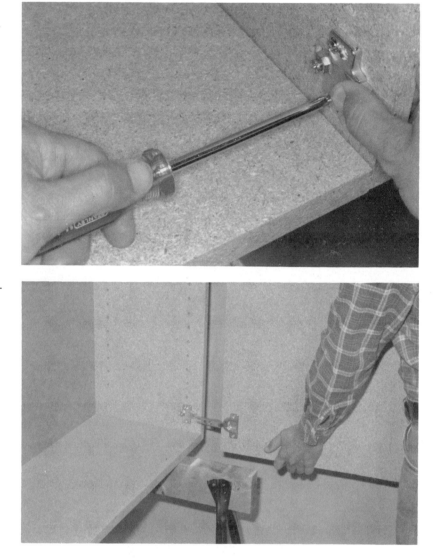

Illus. 3-14. *Slip the door into position and tighten the screws that hold the hinges to the mounting plate. Close the door and check the fit. If the door needs adjustment, turn one of the adjustment screws on the hinge and try closing it again.*

smaller than the screws. Don't drill through to the face of the door. Put some tape on the drill bit to serve as a depth stop. Stop drilling as soon as the tape touches the face of the board.

Install the hinge on the door (Illus. 3-11). Place the cup in the hole and drive the screws into the pilot holes. Temporarily attach the mounting plate to the hinge (Illus. 3-12). Hold the door in position and mark the location of the mounting holes on the side of the cabinet. Drill pilot holes for the screws, and then attach the hinge mounting plate to the side (Illus. 3-13). Slip the door into position and tighten the screws that hold the hinges to the mounting plate.

Close the door and check its fit (Illus. 3-14). If

the door needs adjustment, turn one of the adjustment screws on the hinge and try closing it again (Illus. 3-15).

Measure and mark the location of the door handle (Illus. 3-16). Drill through the door for the handle screws, and then attach the handle with the screws provided. Close the doors and make sure that you're satisfied with the way everything fits, then remove the doors and all of the hardware. After applying the finish, reinstall everything.

The door edges are highly visible with this type of door, so cover the edges with wood-veneer tape before applying a finish (Illus. 3-17). See chapter 5 for details on finishing.

Illus. 3-15. *This type of hinge (adjustable in three directions) is very useful when you have two or more doors in a row. You can adjust the hinges so that all of the doors line up, and there will be an even gap between each door.*

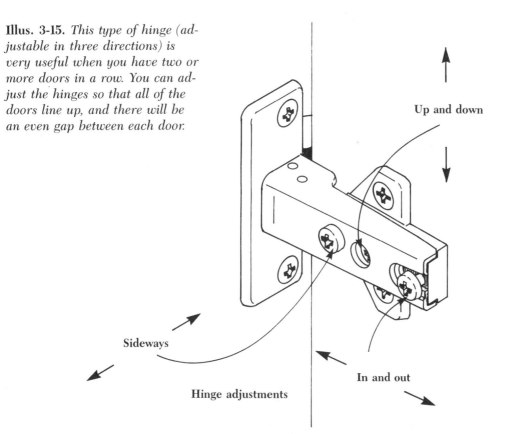

Up and down

Sideways

In and out

Hinge adjustments

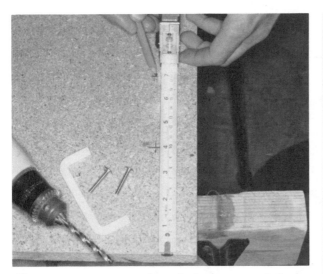

Illus. 3-16. *Measure and mark the location of the door handle. Drill through the door for the handle screws, then attach the handle using the screws provided. Close the doors and make sure that you're satisfied with the way that everything fits, then remove the doors and all of the hardware. After applying the finish, reinstall the doors and hardware.*

Illus. 3-17. *The door edges are highly visible, so cover the edges with wood-veneer tape before finishing. Read chapter 5 for details.*

Style Variations

The type of door I just described gives the cabinet a modern look. If you want a more traditional design, you can add some decorative mouldings to the basic door to simulate a panel door (Illus. 3-18). The panel-door design is popular and it gives a traditional look to a cabinet. A genuine panel door is too complex for a novice cabinetmaker to attempt, but by using mouldings, you can simulate the panel door. There are a large variety of mouldings available that you can apply to a door (Illus. 3-19).

Applying Door-Casing Moulding

Door-casing moulding (Illus. 3-20) is available in pine or a number of other wood varieties, and comes in various widths and styles. There are other similar mouldings that can be used in the same manner. In the illustrations in this section, Philippine mahogany moulding is being applied to a plywood door. If you want to apply moulding to a painted door, you could use pine moulding and a particleboard door.

You'll need two tools that aren't on the basic tool list if you want to apply mouldings to a door: a backsaw and a mitre box (Illus. 3-21).

Cut a mitre on one end of a piece of moulding (Illus. 3-22). A mitre is a 45° cut. Place the moulding flat on the bottom of the mitre box, with the outside edge of the moulding resting against the back of the mitre box. Align the end of the moulding with one of the 45° slots in the mitre box. The mitre cut should be made so that the long point of the joint (on the outside edge of the moulding) slopes in towards the inside edge. Place the saw in the slot and saw through the moulding.

After you've made the first mitre cut on the end of the moulding, place the moulding on the door to mark its length (Illus. 3-23). Align the

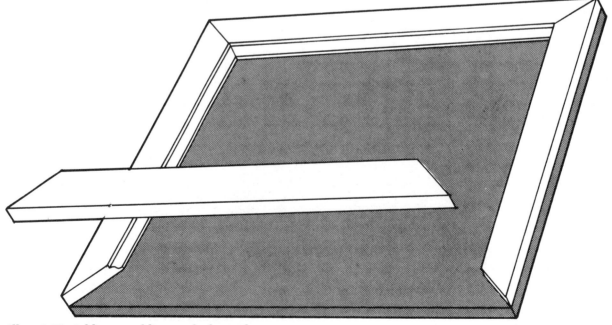

Illus. 3-18. *Adding moulding to the basic door can simulate a traditional panel door.*

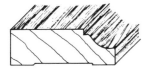

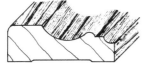
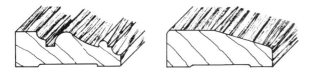

Illus. 3-20. *Standard casing moulding can be used to simulate a panel door.*

Illus. 3-19. *This drawing shows a few of the many different types of mouldings that can be added to a basic door to adapt it to other styles.*

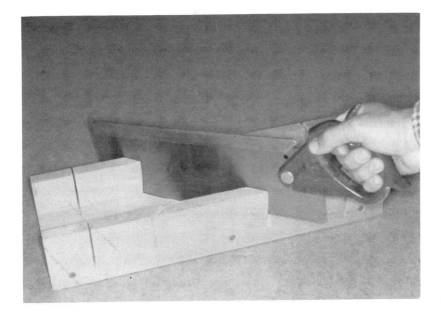

Illus. 3-21. *You'll need a backsaw and a mitre box to cut the mitre joints on the moulding.*

Illus. 3-22. *After you've made the basic door, cut a mitre on one end of a piece of moulding. A mitre is a 45° cut. Place the moulding flat on the bottom of the mitre box with the outside edge of the moulding resting against the back of the mitre box. Align the end of the moulding with one of the 45° slots in the mitre box.*

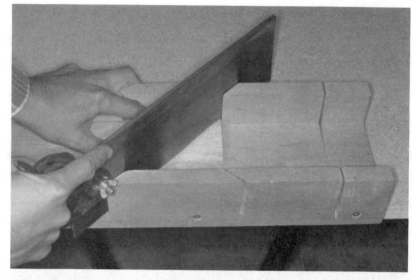

Illus. 3-23. *Now place the moulding on the door to mark the length. Align the point of the mitre with the edge of the door. Mark the other end to indicate where to cut.*

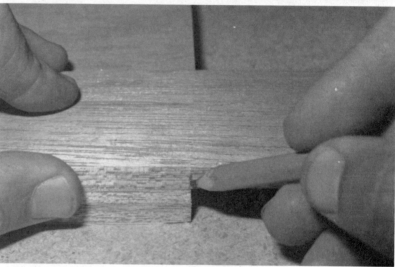

Illus. 3-24. *Put the moulding back in the mitre box and align the mark with the edge of the 45° slot. Make sure that you've positioned the moulding so that the saw kerf will be on the waste side of the line. Put the saw in the slot and saw through the moulding.*

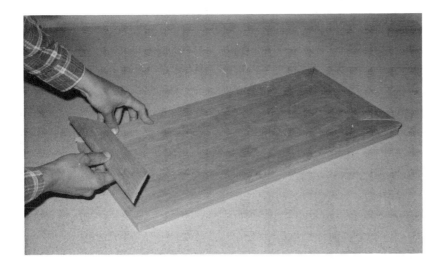

Illus. 3-25. *Repeat the procedure for the other three pieces of moulding, and lay them down on the door to test the fit.*

Illus. 3-26. *Put some glue on the back of one of the pieces of moulding. Align the moulding with the edges of the door and attach the moulding to the door using a few small brads, or finish nails.*

point of the mitre with the edge of the door. Make a mark at the other end to indicate where to cut.

Put the moulding back in the mitre box and align the mark you just made with the edge of the 45° slots (Illus. 3-24). The saw kerf should be on the waste side of the line. Put the saw in the slots and saw through the moulding.

Repeat the procedure for the other three pieces of moulding, and lay them on the door to test their fit (Illus. 3-25).

Put some glue on the back of one of the pieces of moulding (Illus. 3-26). Align the moulding with the edges of the door and attach the moulding, using a few small finishing nails.

Put some glue on the mitre joint and on the back of the next piece of moulding, and then attach it to the door. Repeat this procedure for the other pieces of moulding (Illus. 3-27).

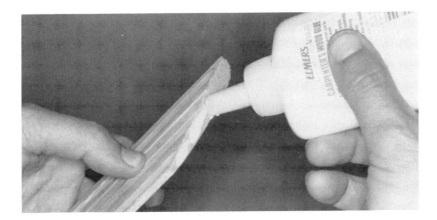

Illus. 3-27. *Put some glue on the mitre joint and to the back of the moulding, then attach it to the door. Repeat this procedure for the rest of the pieces of moulding.*

Illus. 3-28. *Set the nail heads slightly below the surface of the moulding by placing a nail set on the nail head and hitting the set with a hammer. After the nails are set, cover them with putty. When the putty is dry, sand it smooth and the door will be ready to finish.*

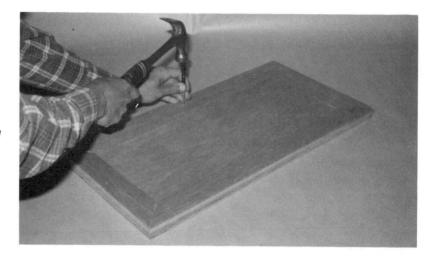

Set the heads of the nails slightly below the surface of the moulding by placing a nail set on the nail head and hitting the set with a hammer (Illus. 3-28). After the nails are set, cover the set holes with putty. When the putty is dry, sand it smooth. The door is now ready for a finish.

Moulding with Curved Corner Pieces

Another type of moulding is especially designed for door decoration. It comes with curved corner pieces (Illus. 3-29). To apply this type of moulding to a cabinet door, first draw a light pencil line where you want the moulding to be placed (Illus. 3-30). Put a piece of moulding in the mitre box and cut a mitre on one end (Illus. 3-31).

Next, temporarily place the corner pieces on the door (Illus. 3-32). Attach them to the door using masking tape. Hold the moulding in place and mark its length.

Cut the mitre on the other end of the moulding where you marked it, and then test-fit the piece on the door (Illus. 3-33). Repeat the procedure for the rest of the pieces. If the joint doesn't fit well, make adjustments to the angle by sanding the end of the moulding with 100-grit sandpaper, wrapped around a block of wood.

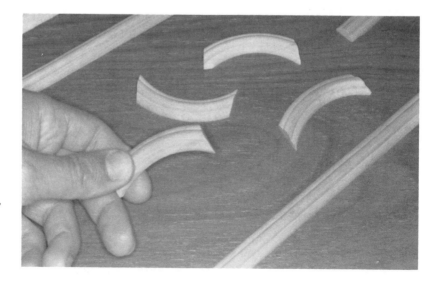

Illus. 3-29. *This type of moulding, specially made for door decoration, comes with curved corner pieces. You can buy several sizes and styles.*

Illus. 3-30. *Begin by drawing a light pencil line to mark the spot where you want to place the moulding.*

Illus. 3-31. *Put a piece of moulding in the mitre box and cut a mitre on one end.*

Now, apply glue to the back of the moulding and permanently attach it to the door (Illus. 3-34). Use a few small brads to secure the moulding to the door. If the moulding starts to split as you drive in the nail, stop and drill a pilot hole using a drill bit that's a bit smaller than the nail. The corner pieces are too fragile to nail. Apply glue to them and hold them in place on the door, using masking tape until the glue sets (Illus. 3-35).

Set the brad heads and then fill them with putty. After the putty is dry, sand it smooth. Now you have a complete door, ready to accept a finish.

Illus. 3-32. *Next, place the corner pieces on the door. Attach them temporarily with masking tape. Hold the side moulding in place and mark the length.*

Illus. 3-33. *Cut the mitre on the end of the moulding where you marked it, then test-fit the piece on the door. Repeat the procedure for the rest of the pieces.*

Applying a Panel

Another way to simulate a panel door is to attach a panel to the surface of the door. This applied panel has curves cut out of the corners (Illus. 3-36). You could also use a panel with square corners.

To make this type of panel, you'll need a sabre saw to cut the curves. You could use a router to

Illus. 3-34. *Now apply glue to the back of the moulding and permanently attach it to the door. Use a few small brads to secure the moulding. Drill pilot holes for the brads if the moulding tends to split.*

Illus. 3-35. *Don't use nails on the corner pieces. Apply glue to the backs, and attach them to the door using masking tape. After the glue is dry, remove the tape. Set the brad heads and fill them over with putty. After the putty is dry, sand it smooth. Now you have a complete door, ready for finishing.*

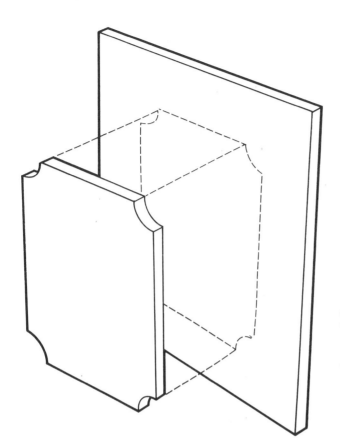

Illus. 3-36. *The applied panel, made from ½"-thick material, is attached to the surface of the basic door. Curved corners and a routed edge can be used decoratively.*

add a decorative edge to the door and the panel. This is optional (Illus. 3-37).

First, determine the size of the panel (Illus. 3-38). Usually, the panel is between 4″ and 6″ smaller than the door, leaving a 2″ to 3″ border around the panel when it's installed. Draw a light pencil line indicating the position of the panel on the door.

Illus. 3-37. *A sabre saw is needed to cut the curved corner on the panel. A router can be used to cut a decorative edge on the panel.*

Illus. 3-38. *The size of the panel is determined by the size of the door and the width of the border around the panel. In this example, the border is 2″, so the panel is 4″ smaller than the door in both dimensions.*

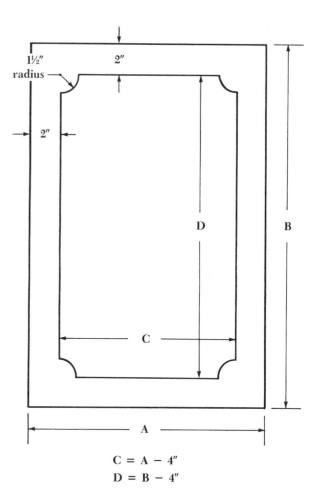

$$C = A - 4″$$
$$D = B - 4″$$

Next, cut the panel from ½″-thick material (Illus. 3-39). Use a guide board and a portable circular saw.

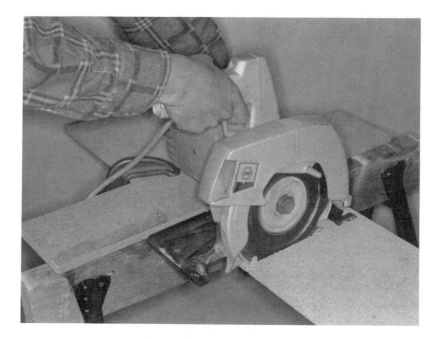

Illus. 3-39. *Cut the panel from ½″-thick material, using a guide board and the portable circular saw.*

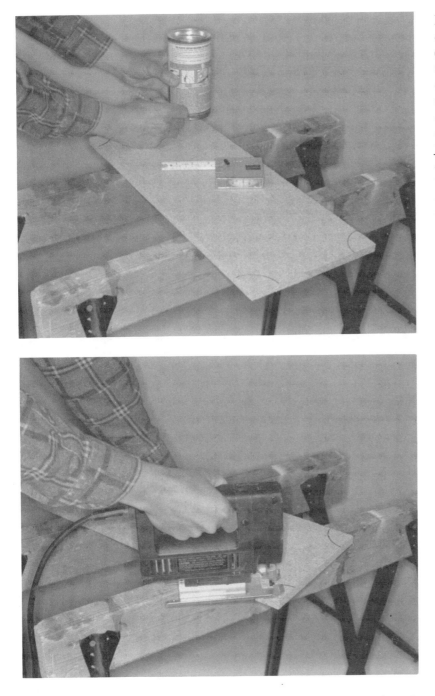

Illus. 3-40. *Now lay out the curves on the panel. Find a can (or other round object) that has the curve you want. Measure an equal distance from the corner of the door along both edges. In this example, the can has a diameter of 3″, and a mark is made 1½″ from the corner on both edges. Align the edge of the can with the marks, and trace around the can. Repeat the procedure on all four corners.*

Illus. 3-41. *Use the sabre saw to cut the curves. Refer to the saw's owner's manual for operating and safety instructions.*

Now, lay out the curves on the panel (Illus. 3-40). Find a metal can (or other round object) that has the type of curve you want. Measure an equal distance from the corner, along both edges. For example, if the can has a diameter of 3″, then make a mark 1½″ from the corner, on both edges. Align the edge of the can with the marks, and then trace around the can.

Use the sabre saw to cut the curves (Illus 3-41). Refer to the saw's owner's manual for operating and safety instructions.

Use a router to add an optional decorative edge to the panel and to the door (Illus. 3-42). Clamp the door panel to a work surface for the routing operation. Use a decorative-edge router bit. There are many bit styles available. The bit

Illus. 3-42. *You can use a router to add a decorative edge to the panel (and to the door, if you choose). Clamp the panel to a work surface for the routing operation. Use a decorative edge bit. The bit, with a pilot that rubs against the edge of the board, will guide the cut. Refer to the router's owner's manual for complete safety and operating instructions. Be sure to use eye protection when you operate a router.*

Illus. 3-43. *The router bit is guided by a pilot that rubs against the edge of the panel, making it easy to follow the curve around the corner.*

has a pilot that rubs against the edge of the board to guide the cut (Illus. 3-43). Refer to the router's owner's manual for complete safety and operating instructions. Use safety goggles when you operate a router.

Apply the panel to the door, using glue and nails (Illus. 3-44). You won't be able to cover the edges with wood-veneer tape if you routed them, so fill the edges following the directions given in chapter 5 (Illus. 3-45).

Illus. 3-44. *Apply the panel to the door with glue and nails.*

Illus. 3-45. *You won't be able to cover the edges with wood-veneer tape if you routed them, so fill the edges following the directions given in chapter 5.*

Chapter 4

DRAWERS

Drawers are usually considered to be a complicated aspect of cabinetmaking, but by using the system described here, you should be able to make drawers without much trouble. The process is simplified because you'll be using dowel joints as well as commercial drawer guides to assemble the drawers (Illus. 4-1).

Building Drawers

Building drawers is a job similar to making a miniature cabinet. The steps are the same, but they must be adapted due to the small size of the parts. The sides and the back of the drawer described here are made from ½"-thick plywood or particleboard. The bottom is made from ⅛" hardboard. Make the front from the same material that you use for the doors.

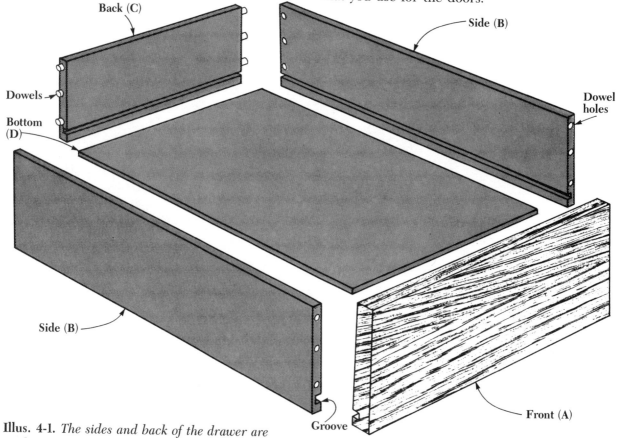

Illus. 4-1. *The sides and back of the drawer are made from ½"-thick plywood or particleboard. The bottom is made from ⅛" hardboard. Make the front from the same material that you use for the doors.*

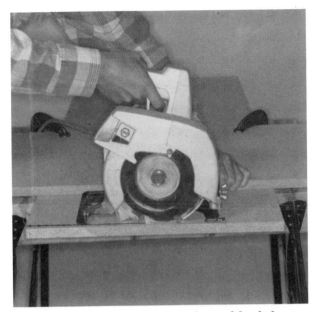

Illus. 4-2. *Before you cut the sides and back from a larger piece, first cut a groove for the bottom. If you wait until after all the parts are cut to size, there won't be enough room on some of the parts to clamp the guide board. Cut the groove all along the length of the sheet to make several drawers. The groove should be ¼" deep and ⅜" up from the bottom edge of the drawer sides.*

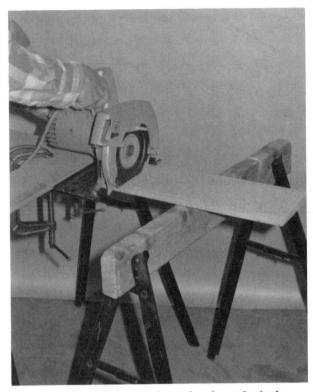

Illus. 4-3. *Cut off a strip from the sheet that's the width needed for the drawer side and the back, and then cut the parts to length.*

Before you cut the sides and back from the larger piece, cut a groove for the bottom (Illus. 4-2). If you wait until after the parts are cut to size, there won't be enough room for you to clamp the guide board. Cut the groove all along the length of the sheet to make several drawers. The groove should be ¼" deep and ⅜" up from the bottom edge of the drawer sides.

Cut off a strip from the sheet that's the width needed for the drawer sides and back, and then cut the parts to length (Illus. 4-3). The length of the sides can be found by measuring the distance inside the cabinet from the back to the front (Illus. 4-4). Make the side ⅜" smaller than this measurement.

Length of drawer sides (**H**) = **A** − ⅜"
Length of back (**I**) = **B** − 2"
Length of drawer front = **C**

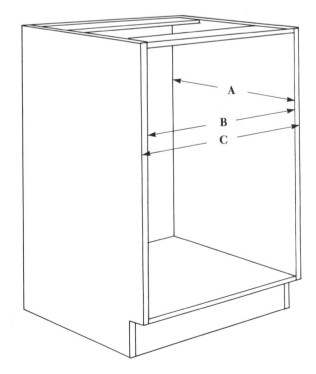

Illus. 4-4. *Measure the cabinet opening to determine the size of the drawer.*

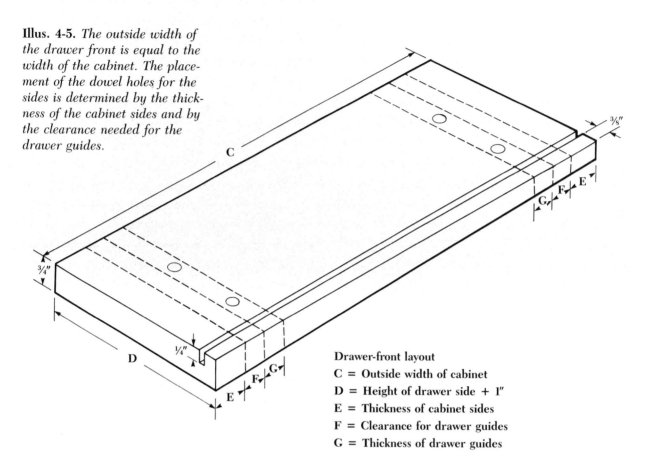

Illus. 4-5. *The outside width of the drawer front is equal to the width of the cabinet. The placement of the dowel holes for the sides is determined by the thickness of the cabinet sides and by the clearance needed for the drawer guides.*

Drawer-front layout

C = Outside width of cabinet

D = Height of drawer side + 1″

E = Thickness of cabinet sides

F = Clearance for drawer guides

G = Thickness of drawer guides

When determining the length of the back, consider the thickness of the sides and the clearance needed for the drawer guides. Most drawer guides will need ½″ clearance on each side of the drawer. Measure the distance from the inside edge of one side of the cabinet to the other inside

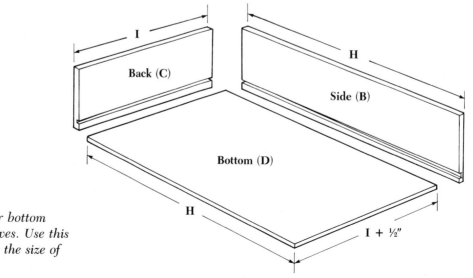

Back (C)

Side (B)

Bottom (D)

Illus. 4-6. *The drawer bottom must fit into the grooves. Use this drawing to determine the size of the bottom.*

edge. Make the drawer back 2″ smaller than this measurement. The 2″ space allows for two ½″-thick sides and two ½″-thick drawer guides.

Cut the front from ¾″-thick material that matches the outside of the cabinet. The front overhangs the sides. Measure the distance between the outside edges of the cabinet to get the length of the drawer front. Make the drawer front 1″ wider than the drawer sides. Cut a groove in the drawer front before cutting it from the larger board. Make the groove ¼″ deep and ⅜″ up from the bottom edge (Illus. 4-5).

Cut the drawer bottom from ⅛″-thick hardboard. The width of the drawer bottom is equal

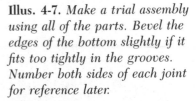

Illus. 4-7. *Make a trial assembly using all of the parts. Bevel the edges of the bottom slightly if it fits too tightly in the grooves. Number both sides of each joint for reference later.*

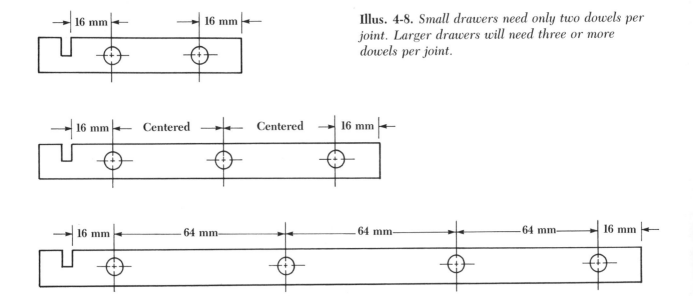

Illus. 4-8. *Small drawers need only two dowels per joint. Larger drawers will need three or more dowels per joint.*

to the length of the back board plus ½″. The length of the drawer bottom is equal to the length of the side board (Illus. 4-6).

Assembly

Make a trial assembly of all the parts (Illus. 4-7). Bevel the edges of the drawer bottom slightly if it fits too tightly in the grooves. Number both sides of each joint for later reference when you drill the dowel joints and make the final assembly.

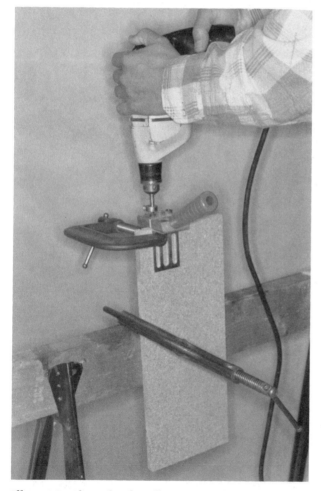

Illus. 4-9. *Place the dowelling jig on the end of the back board (Part C) and line up the ¼″ hole with the layout mark. Clamp the jig in place. Set a depth stop on the bit to make a hole that's 1⅛″ deep. Drill the first hole, then move on to the next hole. Repeat the procedure on the opposite end.*

Use ¼″ dowels to assemble the drawers. Begin with the back. Mark the dowel locations on the ends of the back. For small drawers, you'll need only two dowels. Position the top dowel 16 mm down from the edge. The bottom one should be 16 mm up from the top of the groove. Larger drawers may need a third dowel in the middle. For very large drawers, space the dowels 64 mm apart all along the joint (Illus. 4-8).

Place the dowelling jig on the end of the board and line up the ¼″ hole with the layout mark (Illus. 4-9). Clamp the dowelling jig in place. Set a depth stop on the drill bit to make a hole that's 1⅛″ deep. Drill the hole; then move on the next hole. Repeat the procedure on to the opposite end of the board.

Temporarily insert dowels into the holes in the back (Illus. 4-10). Place it groove-side down. Put the side with the matching joint number groove-side up on top of the back. Position the parts so that the grooves line up. Use C clamps to hold the parts together.

Place the dowelling jig on the board with the slot in the fence over the first dowel. Set the depth stop on the drill to make a ⅜″-deep hole. Drill the first hole, and then move on to the next. Repeat the procedure for the other joint.

Now, lay out the dowel holes for the front joints (Illus. 4-11). Mark the locations on the end of the side boards. The top hole should be 16 mm down from the top, and the bottom hole should be 16 mm up from the top of the groove. If necessary, add more dowels in the middle, spacing them 64 mm apart.

Clamp the dowelling jig in place over the first hole location (Illus. 4-12). Set the depth stop to make a hole 1″ deep. Drill the hole, and then move on to the next location. Repeat the procedure for the other side.

Draw two lines on the back of the drawer front (Illus. 4-13). These lines indicate where the outside of the drawer side will be. You need to allow for the ¾″ thickness of the cabinet sides and the ½″ clearance for the drawer guides, so place the line in 1¼″ from the end of the front.

To drill the dowel holes in the drawer front, remove the guide fence from the dowelling jig

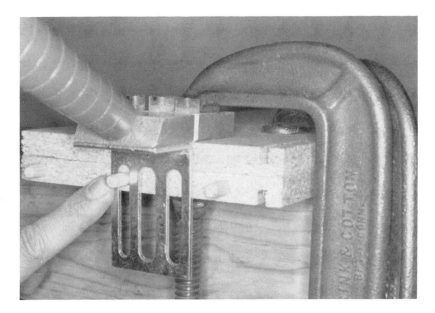

Illus. 4-10. *Temporarily insert dowels into the holes in the back. Place one of the sides (Part B) on top of the back (Part C) and match up the joint numbers. Position the parts so that the grooves line up. Use "C" clamps to hold the parts together. Place the dowelling jig on the top board with the slot in the guide fence over the first dowel. Drill the first hole, then move on to the next. Repeat the procedure for the other joint.*

(Illus. 4-14). The front of the drawer overhangs the sides, so the holes must be placed further in than the fence will allow. A notch in the side of the jig is used for positioning.

Temporarily insert dowels in the holes in the sides (Illus. 4-15). Place the drawer front groove-side up and lay a side on top of it groove-side down. Match the joint numbers and align the

Illus. 4-11. *Now lay out the dowel holes for the front joints. Mark the locations on the end of the side boards. The top hole should be 16 mm down from the top edge, and the bottom hole should be 16 mm up from the top of the groove. If necessary, add more dowels in the middle, spacing them 64 mm apart.*

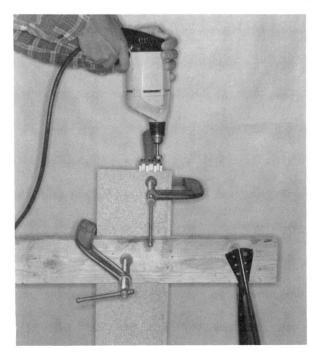

Illus. 4-12. *Clamp the dowelling jig in place over the first hole location. Set the depth stop to make a hole 1″ deep. Drill the hole, and then move on to the next dowel location. Repeat the procedure for the other side.*

Illus. 4-13. *Draw two lines on the back of the drawer front. These lines indicate where the outside of the drawer side will be. Allow space for the ¾" thickness of the cabinet sides and the ½" clearance for the drawer guides, so place the line in from the end of the front 1¼".*

Illus. 4-14. *Remove the guide fence from the dowelling jig to be able to use the jig to drill the holes in the drawer front.*

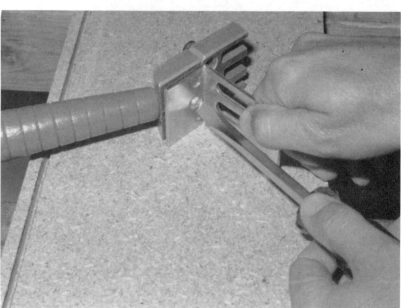

grooves. Put the slot in the dowelling jig over the first dowel. Move the side until the notch in the side of the dowelling jig is on the line you drew on the drawer front (Illus. 4-16). Now, clamp the side to the front.

Set the drill stop to make a ½"-deep hole, and then clamp the dowelling jig in place. Drill the first hole, and then move on to the next dowel location. When you complete this side, remove the first side board and replace it with the second

side board; then repeat the procedure, drilling all the holes for the other side.

Begin assembly by applying a bead of glue to the joint on the back of one side board (Illus. 4-17). Drip some glue into each dowel hole until each hole is about one-third full. Be sure to spread the glue around inside the holes, using a sliver of wood. The ½" sides may split if you drive the dowel in without first spreading the glue.

Insert the dowels into the side, and drive them

Illus. 4-15. *Temporarily insert dowels in the holes in the sides. Place the drawer front face up and lay a side on top of it. Match the joint numbers and align the grooves. Because the front overhangs the sides, the guide fence must be removed from the dowelling jig. Put the slot in the jig over the first dowel. Move the side until the notch in the side of the jig is on the line you drew on the drawer front. Now clamp the side to the front. Clamp the dowelling jig in place. Set the drill stop to make a ½"-deep hole. Drill the first hole, and then move on to the next dowel location. When you've completed this side, remove the side board and replace it with the second side. Repeat the procedure to drill the holes for the other side.*

Illus. 4-16. *Position the dowelling jig by lining up the notch in the side of the jig with a line drawn on the drawer front that indicates the outside of the drawer side.*

all the way in, using a hammer (Illus. 4-18). Apply glue to the mating end of the back board. Drip glue into the dowel holes until they're one-third full of glue, and spread the glue around.

Place the side on the back and align the dowels with the holes. Drive the joint tight with a ham-

mer. Use a scrap of wood against the side to keep the hammer from marking the side (Illus. 4-19).

Put glue into the grooves for the bottom piece. Insert the bottom into the grooves (Illus. 4-20).

Next, assemble the dowel joint to attach the other side to the back (Illus. 4-21). Put glue into

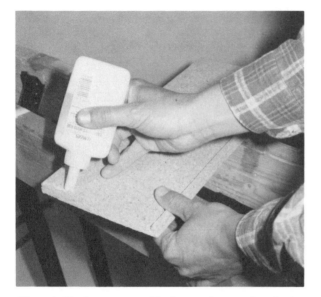

Illus. 4-17. *Begin assembly by applying a bead of glue to the joint on the inside edge of one side board. Drop some glue in each dowel hole and spread the glue around inside the hole.*

Illus. 4-18. *Insert the dowels in the side, and then drive them all the way in, using a hammer.*

the groove for the bottom piece before putting the side in place.

Apply glue to both joints on the drawer front and insert the dowels (Illus. 4-22). Put some glue into the groove for the bottom.

Place the drawer front on the sides. Align the dowels with their holes and start the bottom in its groove. Drive the joints tight (Illus. 4-23).

Measure the diagonals of the drawer to check its squareness (Illus. 4-24). Square it quickly

Illus. 4-19. *Apply glue to the mating end of the back board and to the dowel holes in the back board. Place the side on the back and align the dowels with the holes. Drive the joint tight, using a hammer. Use a scrap of wood against the side to keep the hammer from denting or marking the side.*

Illus. 4-20. *Put some glue in the grooves where the bottom will slip in. Insert the bottom board into the grooves.*

Illus. 4-21. *Next assemble the dowel joint to attach the other side to the back. Put glue in the groove for the bottom before putting this side in place.*

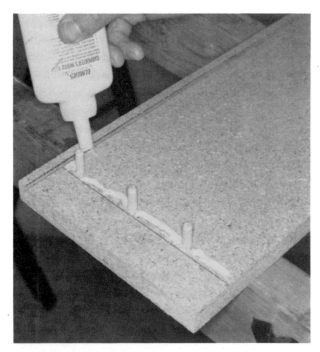

Illus. 4-22. *Apply glue to both joints on the drawer front and insert the dowels. Put some glue in the groove for the bottom.*

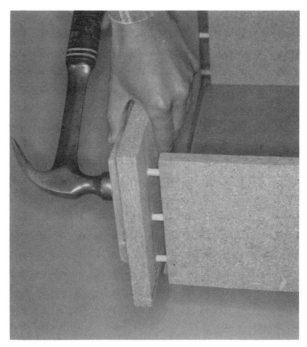

Illus. 4-23. *Place the drawer front on the sides. Align the dowels with their holes and start the bottom in its groove, then drive the joints tight.*

Illus. 4-24. *Measure the diagonals of the drawer to check for squareness. Square up the drawer quickly before the glue has a chance to set. If necessary, clamp the drawer diagonally from corner to corner to pull the drawer square.*

Illus. 4-25. *Apply clamps to the drawer to hold the joints tight as they dry. Leave the clamps in place for at least 1 hour.*

before the glue has a chance to set. If necessary, clamp diagonally from corner to corner to align the drawer so that it's square.

Apply clamps to the drawer to hold the joints tight as they dry (Illus. 4-25). Leave the clamps in place for at least one hour.

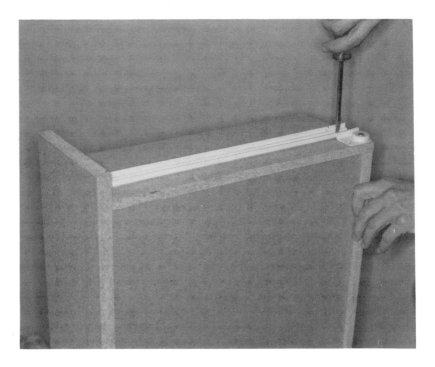

Illus. 4-26. *Attach the drawer guides, following the manufacturer's directions.*

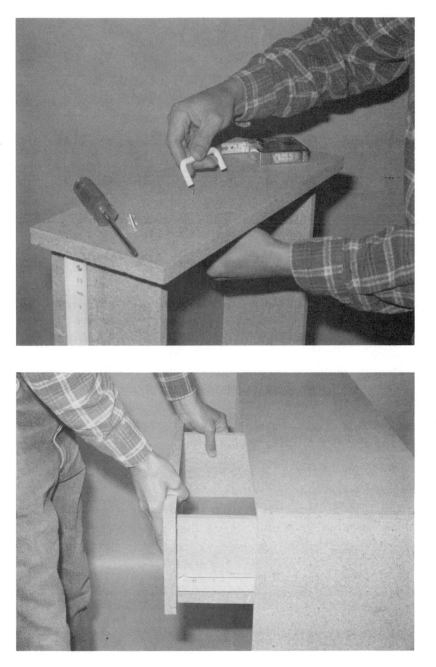

Illus. 4-27. *Drill holes for the drawer pull and then attach it to test the fit.*

Illus. 4-28. *Attach the drawer guides to the sides of the cabinet, following the manufacturer's directions, then test how the drawer fits in the cabinet. After the test, remove all of the hardware before applying the finish.*

Attach the drawer guide, following the manufacturer's directions (Illus. 4-26).

Drill holes for the drawer pull, and attach the pull to test the fit (Illus. 4-27). Attach the drawer guides to the sides of the cabinet, following the manufacturer's directions. Test the drawer in the cabinet (Illus. 4-28). If it fits properly, remove all of the drawer hardware before applying the finish. The groove in the drawer front is visible on the side. You can fill the exposed groove with wood putty before you apply a finish to the drawer. If the drawer front is made from plywood or particleboard, cover the edges with wood-veneer tape before applying a finish. See chapter 5.

APPLYING A FINISH

Applying a finish is one of the most important steps in cabinetry. If you don't give the cabinet a good finish, it won't look attractive, no matter how well you've done the rest of your work. A finish that is done well will make your project look professional.

Cabinets can be stained and varnished, or painted. Lumber and plywood can be given any type of finish, but particleboard is usually painted.

Before applying the finish, prepare the surface by sanding it and filling in rough surfaces. Plywood and particleboard must also have their edges covered.

Wood-Veneer Tape

The raw edges of plywood or particleboard will not take a finish well. Even if you paint them, they'll still look rough.

One of the best ways to hide the raw edges is to cover them with wood-veneer tape, a very thin strip of wood backed with strong paper that comes in a variety of wood types (Illus. 5-1). If you use a stain or varnish, choose veneer tape that's the same species of wood as the face of the plywood. Birch is a good tape to use on particleboard that will be painted.

Cut the tape with scissors, to a length slightly longer than what's needed to cover one edge (Illus. 5-2). Use contact cement to attach the tape. Apply an even coat to the back of the tape and to the edge of the board. Let the cement dry before you proceed (Illus. 5-3).

When the glue is dry, position the tape on the edge. Hold the tape above the board so that it doesn't touch the glue before you're ready (Illus. 5-4). Once the tape touches the board, it sticks to it, so make sure that it's in the proper position before you set it down.

Let about ¼" of the tape overhang the end of the board, and center the tape on the edge so that there's an equal overhang on each side. Press down one end, and then slowly lower the other end as you press the tape in place (Illus. 5-5).

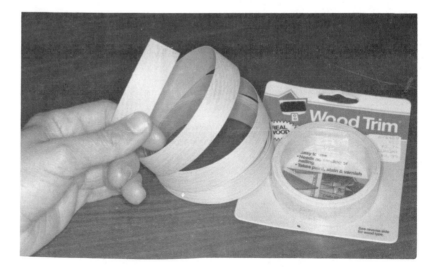

Illus. 5-1. *The raw edges of plywood or particleboard will not hold a finish well. Even if you paint them, they will still look rough. One of the best ways to hide the rough edges is to cover them with wood-veneer tape (a very thin strip of wood backed with strong paper).*

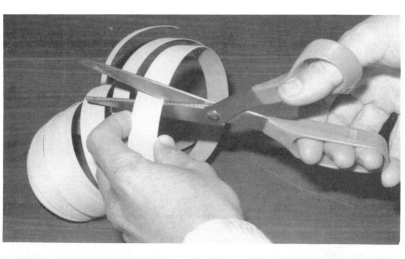

Illus. 5-2. *The tape can be cut with scissors. To cover one edge, cut a length slightly longer than needed.*

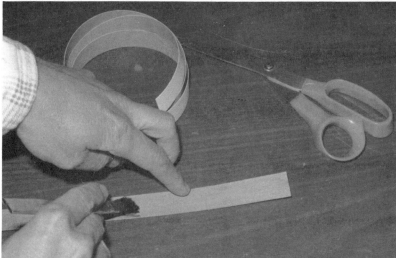

Illus. 5-3. *Use contact cement to attach the tape. Apply an even coat both to the back of the tape and to the edge of the board. Let the cement dry before you proceed.*

Illus. 5-4. *When the glue is dry, position the tape on the edge. Hold the tape above the board so that it doesn't touch the glue before you're ready. Once the tape touches the board, it will stick, so be sure it's in the proper position before you set it down.*

Illus. 5-5. *Press the veneer tape down at one end, then work towards the other end.*

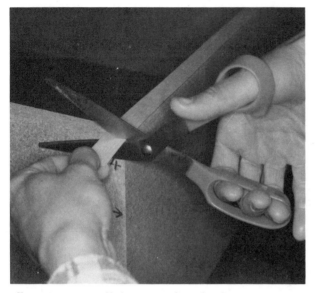

Illus. 5-6. *Cut off the excess length of tape using a pair of scissors.*

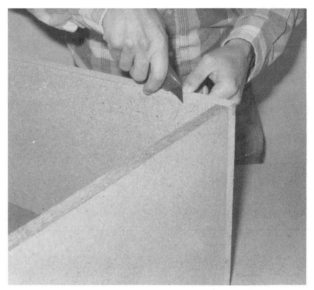

Illus. 5-7. *Use a razor knife to trim the edges flush.*

Rub a block of wood over the tape to press it firmly in place, and then cut off the excess tape with scissors (Illus. 5-6). Use a razor knife to trim the edges flush with the board (Illus. 5-7).

Cut the next strip of tape and apply the glue to the tape and to the edge of the board. Be careful not to get any glue on the strip of tape that's already on the cabinet (Illus. 5-8).

Where two pieces of tape meet at a corner, let the second one overlap the first when you position the tape on the edge. After you've applied the second strip, cut the end off flush with the edge of the first strip. Use a square to guide the utility knife. Place the square against the side of the cabinet and align the blade with the edge of the first strip of tape. Cut through the second strip of tape with the utility knife, guided by the square (Illus. 5-9). After removing the scrap of tape, you should have a good joint (Illus. 5-10).

When all of the tape is in place, sand the edges. Wrap a piece of 100-grit sandpaper around a small block of wood. Sand along the edges of the tape until any overlap left by the knife is removed, then give the edges a slight bevel by holding the sanding block at an angle and sanding the edges. (Illus. 5-11).

Illus. 5-8. *Cut the next strip of tape, and apply the glue both to the tape and to the edge of the board. Be careful not to get any glue on the strip of tape already on the cabinet.*

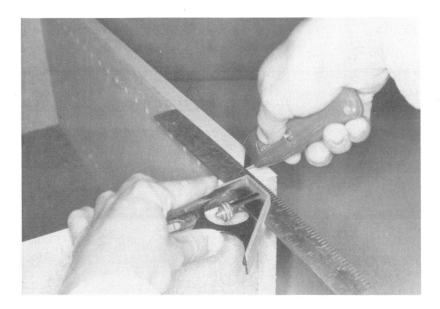

Illus. 5-9. Where two pieces of tape meet at a corner, let the second piece overlap the first one when you position the tape on the edge. After you apply the second strip, cut the end off flush with the edge of the first strip. Use a square as a guide for the utility knife. Place the square against the inside edge of the cabinet and align the blade with the edge of the first strip of tape. Cut through the second strip of tape with the utility knife, guided by the square.

Wood Preparation

Before applying any finish, sand the wood (Illus. 5-12), starting with 100-grit sandpaper. Sand in long, straight strokes *with* the grain of the wood.

When the wood feels smooth, switch to 150-grit sandpaper, and sand again, followed by a final sanding with 180-grit sandpaper.

Hand-sanding can be laborious. Buy a power-sander if you plan on doing a lot of cabinet work (Illus. 5-13).

Illus. 5-10. After removing the scrap of tape, you should have a good joint.

Illus. 5-11. When all of the tape is in place, sand the edges. Wrap a piece of 100-grit sandpaper around a small block of wood. Sand along the edges of the tape until any overlap left by the knife is removed. Give the edges a slight bevel by holding the sanding block at an angle, and then sanding the edges.

Illus. **5-12.** *Before applying any finish, sand the wood. Start with 100-grit sandpaper. Sand in long straight strokes in line with the grain of the wood. When the wood feels smooth, switch to 150-grit and sand the surface again. Then give the surface a final sanding with 180-grit sandpaper.*

Illus. **5-13.** *Hand-sanding can be laborious. Invest in a power sander if you plan on doing a lot of cabinet work.*

Filler

After sanding, remove all of the sanding dust from the surface of the wood. Use a brush, or use a vacuum with a brush attachment (Illus. 5-14).

If you want a very smooth final finish, fill the grain on open-grained woods—oak, Philippine mahogany, and others. Use a paste wood-filler

Illus. **5-14.** *Remove the dust you created during sanding before you proceed with any other finishing steps. A vacuum's brush attachment works well.*

Illus. 5-15. *If you want a very smooth final finish, fill the grain on open-grained woods (like oak and Philippine mahogany). Use a paste wood-filler. Paste wood-filler is also used on particleboard to make the surface smooth enough to paint well.*

(Illus. 5-15). Don't confuse wood-filler with the wood putty that's used to fill nail holes. A paste wood-filler is used to fill tiny pores in the wood surface.

Paste wood-filler is also used on particleboard to make the surface smooth enough to accept a good paint job. If you've tried painting particleboard without filling the surface, you know that the result is usually a rough surface, no matter how many coats of paint you use. Paste wood-

filler is used by professionals to get a smooth finish on particleboard. Fill particleboard as you would fill open-grained hardwoods.

Most paste wood-fillers come in a concentrated form that must be thinned before use. Follow the directions on the can for mixing the paste with thinner (Illus. 5-16).

Use a brush to apply the filler (Illus. 5-17). If you didn't cover the edges of the particleboard with veneer tape, be sure to give them a good coat of filler. Let the filler dry as specified in the directions on the can, and then wipe it off with a cloth. Use a circular motion as you wipe (Illus. 5-18). Cheesecloth or burlap both work well, because of the coarse texture of the cloth.

Let the filler dry for another 15 minutes, and then wipe off the residue with a clean cloth. Let the filler dry overnight, and then go over the surface lightly with fine steel wool (Illus. 5-19).

Illus. 5-16. *Most paste wood-fillers are concentrated, and they must be thinned before use. Follow the directions on the can for mixing the paste with thinner.*

Illus. 5-17. *Apply the paste wood-filler with a brush. If you didn't cover the edges of the particle-board with veneer tape, be sure to give the edges a good coat of filler.*

Applying a Stain

Remove all of the sanding dust from the board's surface, using a brush or a vacuum cleaner before you apply a stain.

Apply the stain using a foam brush. The foam brush gives better results than does a bristle brush, because it holds more stain, and it distributes it evenly. Brush the stain on in long, even strokes *with* the grain (Illus. 5-20).

Let the stain stay on the wood for a while. Wipe the wood with a cloth to remove the excess stain and to even out the color (Illus. 5-21). Follow the directions on the can for the exact procedure to follow for the particular type of stain

Illus. 5-18. *Let the filler dry (as specified in the directions on the can), then wipe off the excess with cheesecloth, using a circular motion.*

Illus. 5-19. *Let the filler dry (completely) overnight, then "sand" it lightly, using fine steel wool.*

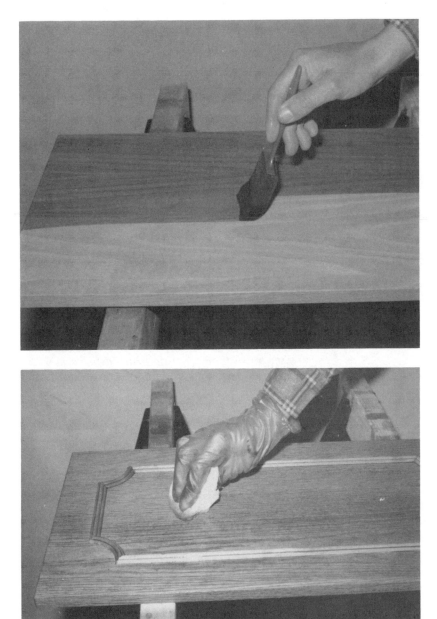

Illus. 5-20. *Apply the stain, using a foam brush. The foam brush will actually give better results than a bristle brush will, because the foam brush holds more stain and distributes the stain evenly. Brush the stain on in long, even strokes, following the direction of the grain.*

Illus. 5-21. *Let the stain sit on the wood for a while, then wipe it with a cloth to remove the excess and even out the color.*

you are using. Let the stain dry before you apply the varnish.

Applying Varnish

Use a polyurethane varnish that's compatible with the stain you used. Try to use the same brand of stain and varnish.

Remove any dust that settled on the wood surface, using either tack cloth or a vacuum cleaner. Tack cloth is a specially treated piece of sticky cheesecloth that traps the dust (Illus. 5-22). You can buy tack cloth at most stores that sell wood-finishing supplies.

Use a new foam brush to apply the varnish, since the foam brush will give a smoother finish than does a bristle brush—it leaves fewer brush marks. Apply the varnish in long, steady strokes

Illus. 5-22. *Remove any dust that has settled on the surface of the wood with a tack cloth (a specially treated sticky piece of cheesecloth that traps the dust).*

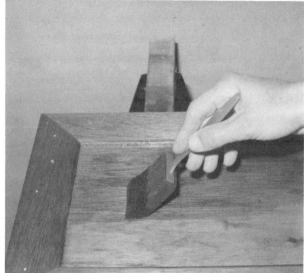

Illus. 5-23. *Use a polyurethane varnish that's compatible with the stain you used. Apply the varnish using a new foam brush. The foam brush will give a smoother finish than a bristle brush will, because it leaves fewer brush marks. Apply the varnish in long, steady strokes in the direction of the grain. Cover the wood completely, but don't put on a heavy coat. A heavy coat will sag and run. It's better to apply several thin coats.*

with the grain (Illus. 5-23). Cover the wood completely, but don't apply a heavy coat that will sag and run. Apply several thin coats, instead.

Let the varnish dry for the length of time specified on the can. Sand the varnish lightly between coats, using 220-grit sandpaper. Wipe off the sanding dust using a tack cloth, and then apply another coat of varnish.

Paint

For small projects, spray paint produces professional results. For larger projects, brush on the paint, or use a spray gun that you can rent or buy (Illus. 5-24). If you paint particleboard, don't use latex paint, or any other water-based paint. The water soaks into the surface, making it bumpy.

Apply a primer before you apply the finish coats. The primer seals the wood and fills minor surface irregularities. Remove dust from the wood, using a tack cloth or a vacuum cleaner, before you apply the primer. After the primer is dry, sand thoroughly with 220-grit sandpaper.

Illus. 5-24. *For small projects, spray paint produces professional results. For larger projects, use a spray gun.*

Illus. 5-25. *To apply paint with a spray can, use long, straight strokes and keep the can about 6" from the surface. For recoating, follow the directions on the can. Usually three light coats will produce a good finish.*

Remove the sanding dust, using a vacuum, and then wipe a tack cloth over the surface to remove any remaining dust.

Apply the first coat of paint. If you use a spray, use long, straight strokes and keep the can about 6" from the surface (Illus. 5-25). Follow the directions found on the can if you recoat. Three light coats usually produce a good finish.

Chapter 6

FREESTANDING CABINETS

You can build virtually any type of freestanding cabinet you want, using the frameless system. You can build anything, from a small bookcase to a china hutch, by using the same construction. In the frameless system, large projects are made from smaller modules. By varying the size of the modules and the ways you combine them, you can make many designs. Two basic modules are used in freestanding cabinets: the base module and the shelf module. In this chapter, you'll learn to make three different-size modules that can be combined to make a variety of projects (Illus. 6-1).

The base module is designed to rest on the floor, and the shelf module is designed to rest atop a base module. The base module can be

Illus. 6-1. *You can build virtually any type of free-standing cabinet you want using the frameless system. Very large projects can be made using smaller modules. Three different-size modules were used to make all of the cabinets shown here.*

Illus. **6-2.** *The base module rests on the floor; the shelf module rests atop the base module. The base module can be used alone in projects such as a TV stand or a small bookcase.*

used alone to make a TV stand or a small bookcase (Illus. 6-2). A base module can have doors or you could add drawers.

The shelf module can't stand alone, so it's only used as the upper section of projects like a china hutch, a large bookcase or an entertainment center (Illus. 6-3).

Modules can be placed side-by-side to make wide projects, like the unit shown in Illus. 6-1, or they can be used individually.

Base Module

A base module rests on the floor. The bottom shelf is raised off the floor 4". The space below the shelf is boxed in by a board called the "toe-kick" (Illus. 6-4). The height of a base module can be varied. The width of the module should not be greater than 36". If you need a wider cabinet, build two modules and place them side-by-side. The modules I build are 29" high, 15" deep and 36" wide (Illus. 6-5). This is a good size for many uses.

Illus. **6-3.** *The shelf module is not designed to stand alone. It's only used as the upper section of projects such as a china hutch, a large bookcase or an entertainment center.*

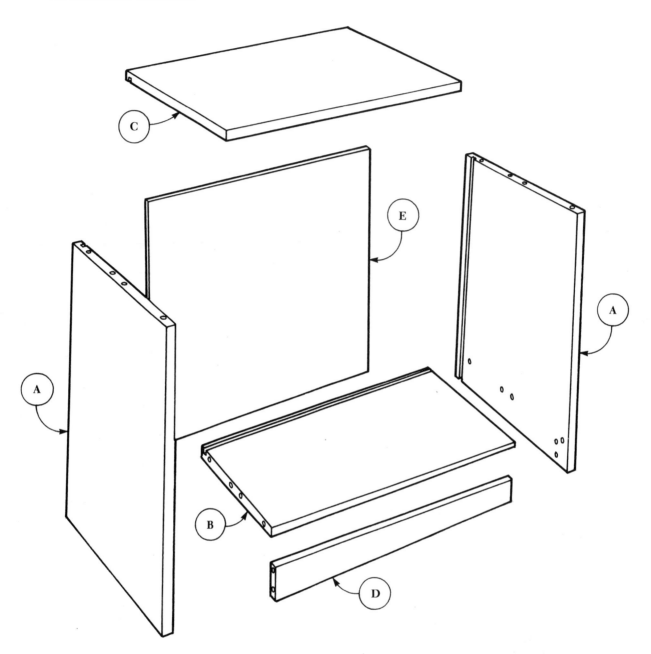

Illus. 6-4. *A base module is designed to rest on the floor. The bottom shelf is raised off the floor 4″. The space below the shelf is boxed in by a board called the "toe-kick." See the Bill of Materials on page 94.*

A module taller than 4′ requires a fixed shelf in the center to add rigidity to the cabinet (Illus. 6-6).

Most of the construction follows the same procedures described in chapter 2 (Illus. 6-7 and 6-8). However, the instructions for the bottom shelf and for the fixed center shelf are different (Illus. 6-9). To make the dowel joints for these shelves, begin by marking the location of the shelf on the inside face of the sides. Draw a line

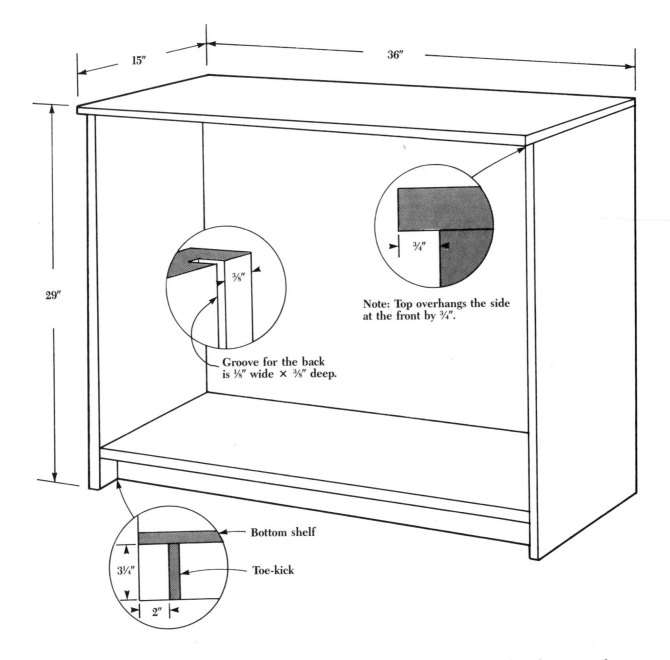

Illus. 6-5. *You can vary the height of a base module. The width of the module should not be greater than 3′. The dimensions shown here can be used to make the modules for the cabinets shown in Illus. 6-1.*

indicating the bottom of the shelf. Number the joints on both the side and the shelf.

Next, drill the dowel holes in the ends of the bottom shelf, as usual (Illus. 6-10 and 6-11). Temporarily place dowels in the holes in the ends of

the shelf. Place the shelf on top of the side. Align the grooves. Remove the guide fence from the dowelling jig. Place the slot in the jig over the first dowel. Slide the shelf back and forth until the notch in the side of the dowelling jig is on the

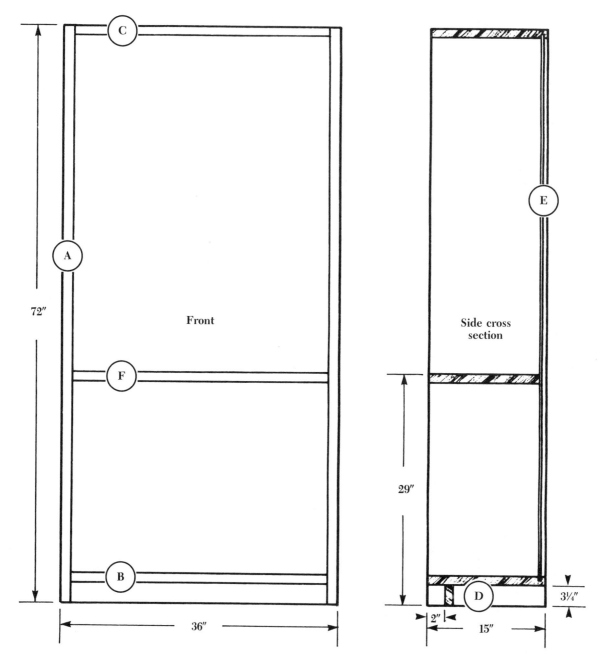

Illus. 6-6. *A tall module is taller than 4'. A tall module requires a fixed shelf in the middle to add rigidity to the cabinet. These are the dimensions for the tall module shown in Illus. 6-1.*

line (Illus. 6-12), then clamp the boards together and drill the holes, as usual (Illus. 6-13).

If you're making a tall module with a fixed middle shelf, the procedure for drilling the holes is similar to the procedure just described for the bottom, except that the shelf will be narrower than the side, and there is no groove in the shelf. When you place the shelf on the side to guide the dowelling jig, align the front of the shelf with the front edge of the side.

Illus. 6-7. *Cut the parts to size using a portable circular saw. Mark the parts layout on the sheet of particleboard and then position the guide board. Offset the guide board from the layout line by the distance between the edge of the saw base and the saw blade. Clamp the guide board in place and make the cut.*

Illus. 6-8. *Use the circular saw to cut a groove for the back. The groove is set back ⅜" from the back of the cabinet. Make the groove ⅛" wide and ⅜" deep. Clamp a guide board in place to guide the saw.*

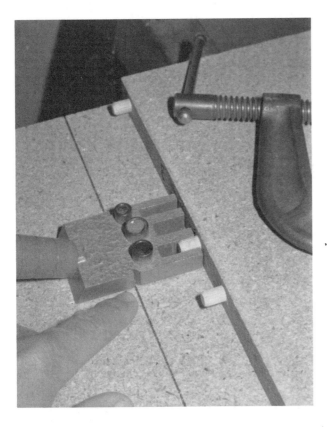

The toe-kick board is attached to the sides, using dowels. The board can be flush with the front of the cabinet, or recessed back, up to 2" (Illus. 6-14). After drilling the holes in the ends of the toe-kick board (Illus. 6-15), temporarily put dowels in the holes and use the toe-kick as a guide for the dowelling jig when drilling the mating holes in the side. Place the toe-kick on the

Illus. 6-9. *Most of the construction follows the same procedures shown in chapter 2. However, the procedures for the bottom shelf and for the fixed middle shelf are different. To make the dowel joints for these shelves, start by making a line indicating the bottom of the shelf. Temporarily put dowels in the holes in the shelf. Place the shelf on top of the side. Remove the guide fence from the dowelling jig. Place the slot in the jig over a dowel. Slide the shelf back and forth until the notch in the side of the dowelling jig is on the line, and then clamp the boards together.*

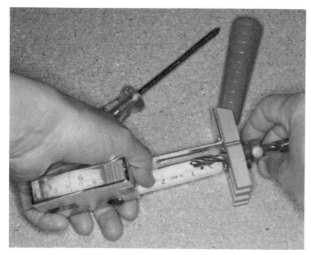

Illus. 6-10. *Set up the dowelling jig to drill ⁵⁄₁₆″ holes that are 1⅛″ deep. This setting is used to drill the holes in the top end of the sides.*

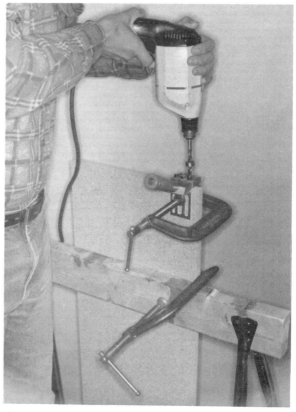

Illus. 6-11. *On the base module, the top overhangs the sides. The joint is oriented differently from the one that was shown in chapter 1. Drill the holes in the ends of the sides (Part A) first, then use the sides to guide the jig as you drill ½″-deep holes in the bottom of the top board (Part C).*

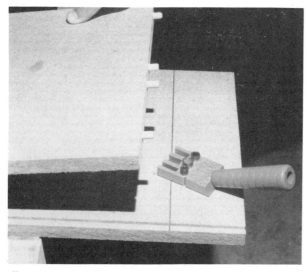

Illus. 6-12. *Drill 1⅛″-deep holes in the ends of the bottom shelf (Part B) and temporarily insert dowels in the holes. Now use the shelf to guide the jig as you drill the holes in the sides (Part A).*

Illus. 6-13. *The guide fence must be removed from the dowelling jig before drilling the holes for the bottom shelf. Draw a line on the inside face of the side (Part A) that indicates the bottom of the shelf. Place the dowelling jig so that the notch in the side is on the line. Clamp the shelf in place and use it to guide the dowelling jig as you drill the ½″-deep holes in the sides.*

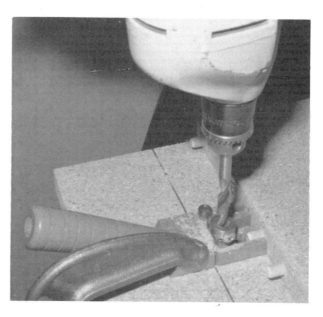

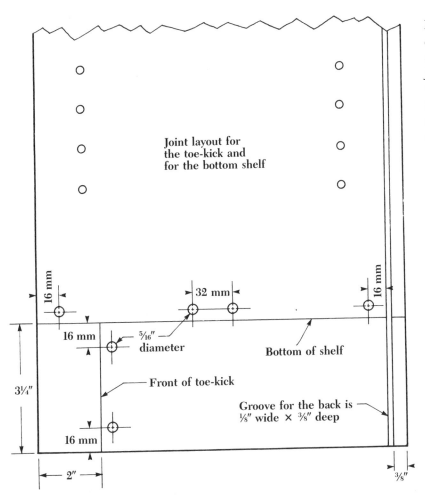

Illus. 6-14. *The toe-kick board is attached to the sides using dowels. It can be flush with the front of the cabinet or it can be recessed up to 2″ back. This plan shows the location of the toe-kick and the bottom shelf for the cabinets shown in Illus. 6-1.*

Joint layout for the toe-kick and for the bottom shelf

16 mm

32 mm

16 mm

16 mm

⁵⁄₁₆″ diameter

Bottom of shelf

Front of toe-kick

Groove for the back is ⅛″ wide × ⅜″ deep

3¼″

16 mm

2″

⅜″

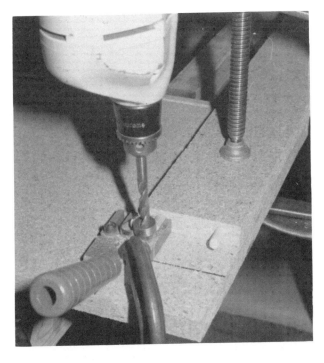

side. Remove the fence from the dowelling jig and place the slot in the jig over the first dowel. Slide the toe-kick back and forth until the notch in the side of the dowelling jig lines up with the layout line that indicates the location of the front of the toe-kick. Clamp the toe-kick to the side. Now drill the holes in the side.

Illus. 6-15. *Drill 1⅛″-deep holes in the ends of the toe-kick board (Part D). Temporarily insert dowels in the holes and use them to guide the dowelling jig as you drill ½″-deep holes in the sides (Part A). The guide fence is removed from the jig for this operation, and a line indicating the front of the toe-kick is used to position the jig.*

Illus. 6-16. *Use the 2 × 4 jig (described in chapter 2) to drill the adjustable-shelf holes in the sides.*

Illus. 6-17. *Assemble the cabinet. Begin with the bottom shelf and the toe-kick. Put the back in the groove before you add the second side. Be sure to glue the back in its groove.*

Illus. 6-18. *Attach the top last. Notice that the front edge of the top overhangs the side by ¾". This detail hides the top of the doors or the drawers.*

Illus. 6-19. *Square up the cabinet and then clamp the joints using bar clamps. Let the glue dry for at least one hour before removing the bar clamps.*

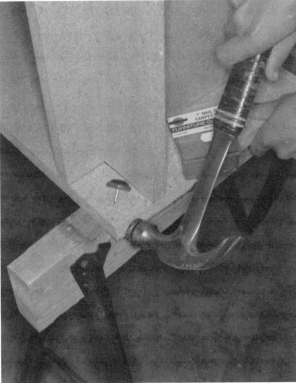

Illus. 6-20. *When the cabinet is finished, attach furniture glides to the bottom. The glides protect the floor and the cabinet and make the cabinet more stable on an uneven floor.*

Assembly procedures are similar to those described in chapter 2 (Illus. 6-16 through 6-19). Make sure to put the toe-kick in before you attach the second side.

Tack furniture glides (Illus. 6-20) to the bottom of the sides; they'll protect the floor, they'll keep the bottom of the cabinet from getting chipped, and they'll prevent rocking on an uneven floor.

Shelf Modules

A shelf module rests atop a base module. The shelf can be the same width and depth as the base module, or you could make it smaller. The construction is essentially the same as that shown in chapter 2 (Illus. 6-21). The modules built here are 43″ tall, 12″ deep and 36″ wide. The groove for the back is set back ⅜″, leaving 11½″ of usable shelf width (Illus. 6-22). Construction is shown in Illus. 6-23 through 6-30.

Illus. 6-21. *A shelf module is designed to sit on top of a base module. This drawing shows a basic shelf module. The letters refer to the Bill of Materials, at the end of this chapter.*

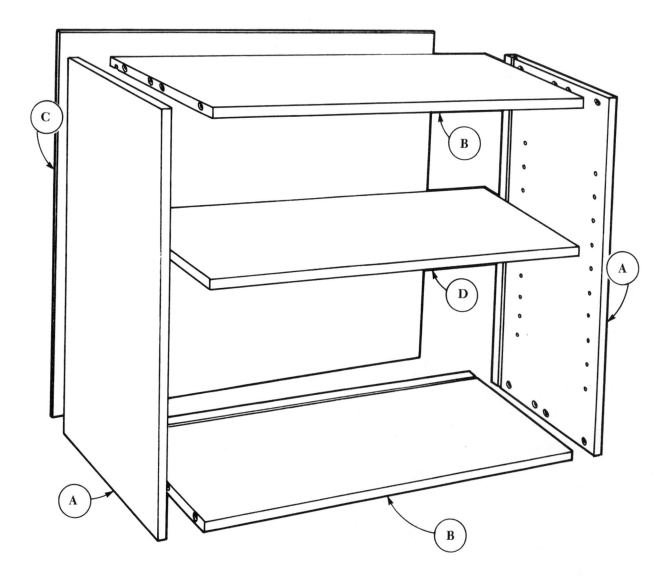

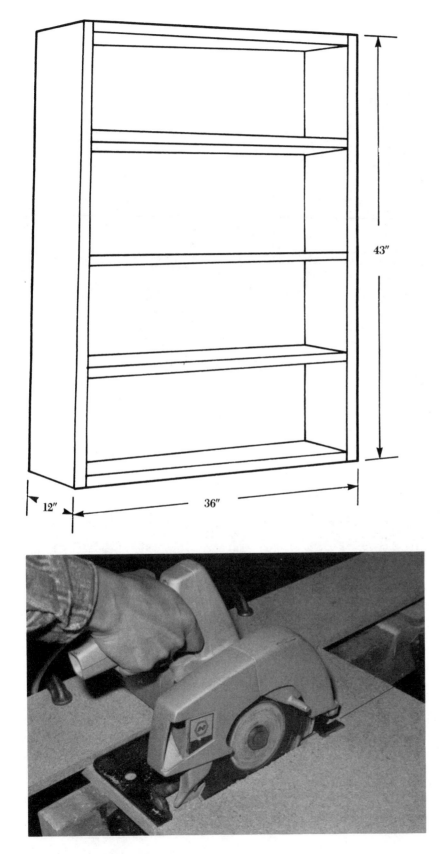

Illus. 6-22. *This plan gives the dimensions used to make the shelf module shown in Illus. 6-1.*

43"

12"   36"

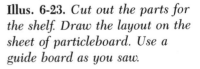

Illus. 6-23. *Cut out the parts for the shelf. Draw the layout on the sheet of particleboard. Use a guide board as you saw.*

Illus. 6-24. *Cut a ⅛″-wide by ⅜″-deep groove for the back. The groove is set back ⅜″ from the back edge of the cabinet.*

After constructing both modules, place the shelf module atop the base module. Use clamps to temporarily hold them together. Drive screws up through the top of the base module into the bottom of the shelf module (Illus. 6-31).

Illus. 6-25. *Lay out the dowel locations on the end of the bottom board (Part B). Drill ⁵⁄₁₆″ diameter by 1⅛″-deep holes for the dowels. Use the bottom board as a guide for the holes in the top board by temporarily inserting dowels in the holes in the bottom board and then clamping the two boards together. Change the depth setting to make ½″-deep holes, and then drill the holes in the sides, using the dowels in the mating boards to guide the jig.*

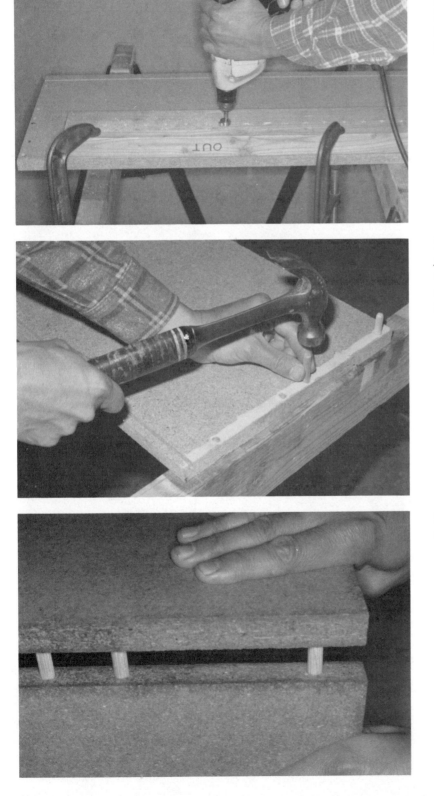

Illus. 6-26. *Use the 2 × 4 jig (described in chapter 2) to guide the drill as you make the ¼"-diameter holes for the adjustable shelves. Set the drill stop to make the holes ½" deep.*

Illus. 6-27. *Apply glue to the joints and spread it around inside the dowel holes. Drive the dowels into the first joint in the side (Part A).*

Illus. 6-28. *Next, attach the bottom (Part B) to the side.*

Illus. 6-29. *Put glue in the groove for the back and then slip the back (Part C) into place.*

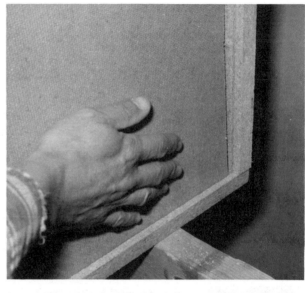

Illus. 6-30. *Attach the top and the other side, then square up the cabinet and then clamp the joints with bar clamps. Leave the clamps in place for at least one hour as the glue dries.*

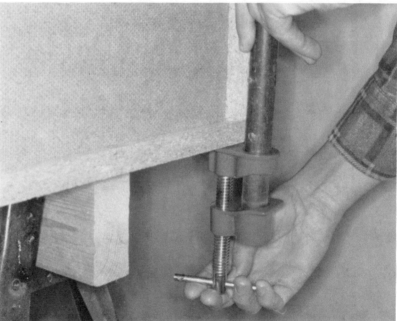

Style Variations

The basic frameless style produces the clean, simple lines of the European-style cabinet. The hutch shown here is made from one short base module and one shelf module. Basic slab doors and simple door pulls keep the lines simple (Illus. 6-32).

Adding different types of doors and trim can transform a frameless cabinet. The next two examples use the same basic modules, but by adding some trim to the doors and to the top of the cabinet, the style changes.

Adding an applied panel to the doors and a cornice moulding to the top help to give the cabinet a traditional look (Illus. 6-33). The applied panel is described in chapter 3. The cornice is

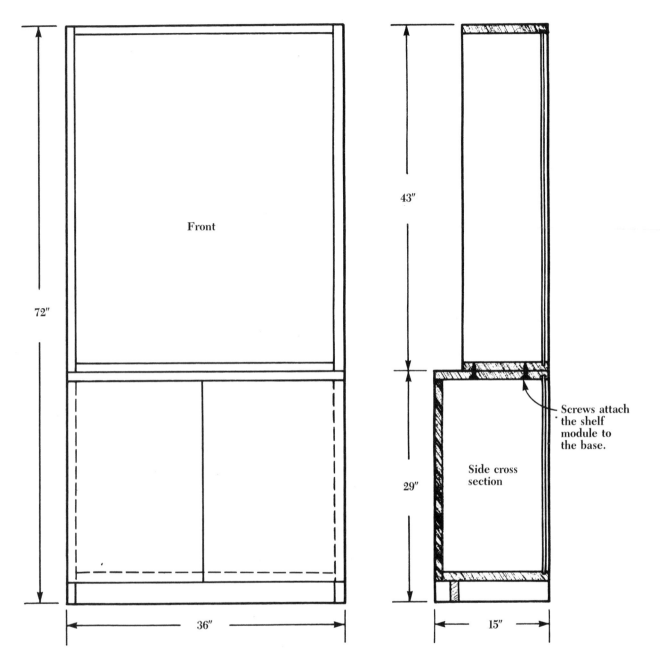

Illus. 6-31. *After constructing both modules, place the shelf module atop the base module. Use clamps to temporarily hold them together. Drive screws up through the top of the base module and into the bottom of the shelf module. This is a drawing of the hutch shown in Illus. 6-1.*

made from standard moulding that's available at most lumberyards.

Cut the cornice moulding in a mitre box. Place the moulding so that the flat edges at the top and the bottom, both rest against the box. This places the moulding at the same angle it will be when it's installed (Illus. 6-34). Attach the cornice moulding to the top of the cabinet, using finish nails and glue (Illus. 6-35).

For an Early-American style cabinet, add some moulding to the doors and some "gingerbread" to the top of the cabinet (Illus. 6-36). A

Illus. 6-32. *The basic frameless style produces the clean simple lines of the European-style cabinet. Adding different types of doors and trim can adapt the frameless cabinet to other styles.*

Illus. 6-33. *Applied panels on the doors and a cornice moulding on top of the shelf give this cabinet a traditional look.*

board with a fancy edge is called "gingerbread." You could change the look of the cabinet depending upon the type of gingerbread you choose (Illus. 6-37). Transfer the pattern to the board. The patterns shown in Illus. 6-38 are sized for a 36"-wide cabinet.

Enlarge the pattern onto a piece of paper. Fold the paper in half and draw the pattern so that the

center line is on the fold. Each square on the drawing is equal to a 1"-square on the full-size pattern. To enlarge the pattern, draw 1"-squares on the paper to use as a guide as you draw. Count the squares to the peaks and valleys on the pattern and mark the location on the full-size drawing. Connect the marks with curved lines that resemble the lines in the pattern. You can also

Illus. 6-34. *Cut the cornice moulding in a mitre box. Place the moulding so that the flat edges at the top and at the bottom rest against the box; this places the moulding at the same angle it will be in when it's installed.*

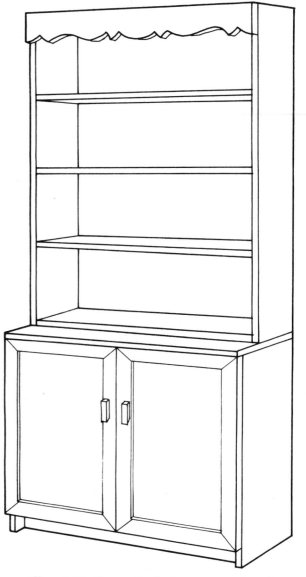

Illus. 6-35. *Attach the cornice moulding using finish nails and glue.*

Illus. 6-36. *For an Early American-style cabinet, use moulding on the doors and then add some "gingerbread."*

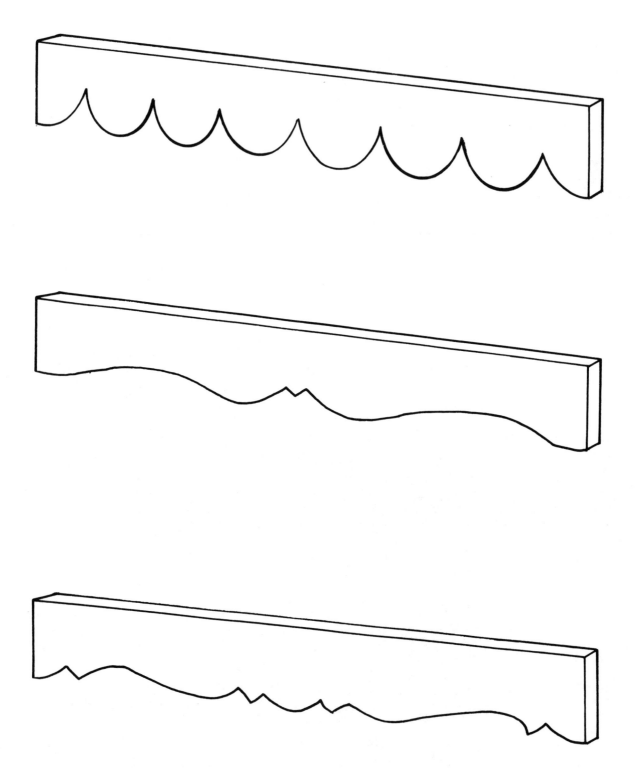

Illus. 6-37. *A board with a fancy edge is called "gingerbread." You can change the look of a cabinet, depending on the type of gingerbread you choose.*

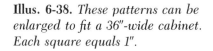

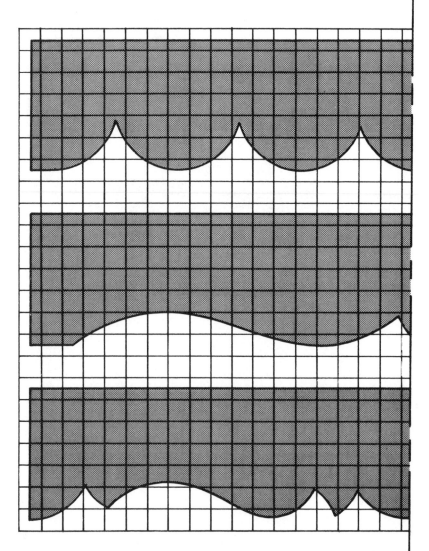

Illus. 6-38. *These patterns can be enlarged to fit a 36"-wide cabinet. Each square equals 1".*

Illus. 6-39. *You need a sabre saw to cut the "gingerbread." Draw the outline on the board, then follow the line with the sabre saw.*

use a photocopier to enlarge the patterns. Adjust the enlargement factor until the squares are one inch in the final copy. You'll need to copy the pattern in sections and then tape them together. When you have the pattern drawn, cut it out with scissors and then unfold the paper. This will give you the complete pattern. Place the paper pattern on the board and trace around it.

Use a sabre saw to cut the "gingerbread." Study the saw's operating manual to find complete directions. Make relief cuts (straight cuts in from the edge of the board through the waste) for some of the tight angles. After making the relief cuts, follow the drawn line with the sabre saw (Illus. 6-39).

When you've cut out the design, sand the rough edges, then attach the "gingerbread" to the top of the cabinet, using glue and finish nails (Illus. 6-40).

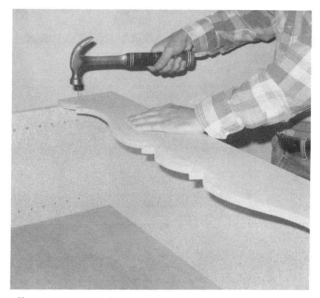

Illus. 6-40. *Attach the "gingerbread" to the top of the cabinet, using glue and finish nails.*

Bill of Materials

The following lists give the sizes for each part of the three types of freestanding cabinet modules shown in Illus. 6-1. The letters refer to the labels on Illus. 6-4, 6-6, and 6-21. All dimensions are actual, in inches.

CABINET TYPE: BASE
SIZE: 29″ high × 36″ wide × 15″ deep
REFER TO ILLUS. 6-4

PART	DESCRIPTION	SIZE	NO. REQ'D
A	sides	¾ × 28¼ × 14¼	2
B	bottom	¾ × 34½ × 14¼	1
C	top	¾ × 36 × 15	1
D	toe-kick	¾ × 34½ × 3¼	1
E	back	⅛ × 25 × 35¼	1
F	doors	¾ × 18 × 25	2

CABINET TYPE: TALL BASE
SIZE: 72″ high × 36″ wide × 15″ deep
REFER TO ILLUS. 6-6

PART	DESCRIPTION	SIZE	NO. REQ'D
A	sides	¾ × 72 × 15	2
B	bottom	¾ × 34½ × 15	1
C	top	¾ × 34½ × 15	1
D	toe-kick	¾ × 34½ × 3¼	1
E	back	⅛ × 35¼ × 71¼	1
F	center shelf	¾ × 35¼ × 14½	1
G	other shelves	¾ × 35⅛ × 14½	varies

CABINET TYPE: SHELF
SIZE: 43″ high × 36″ wide × 12″ deep
REFER TO ILLUS. 6-21

PART	DESCRIPTION	SIZE	NO. REQ'D
A	sides	¾ × 43 × 12	2
B	top & bottom	¾ × 34½ × 12	1
C	back	⅛ × 35¼ × 42¼	1
D	shelf	¾ × 34⅜ × 11½	varies

Chapter 7
BUILT-IN CABINETS

Built-in cabinets are usually associated with kitchens (Illus. 7-1) and bathrooms, although they can also be used in other rooms. They're very useful in a laundry room or a garage. You can build any of these built-in cabinets using the frameless system. If you're a novice cabinet-maker I don't recommend that you build a complete set of kitchen cabinets as your first project, but an overhead cabinet for a laundry room is a good beginner's project.

The principles of construction are the same for all built-in cabinets. There are just two basic modules: the overhead module (Illus. 7-2), and the base module (Illus. 7-3). There are a few basic sizes for most built-in modules (Illus. 7-4). You can make a unit to fit almost any application by combining these standard-size modules. For special applications, vary the size of the modules.

Illus. 7-1. *Built-in cabinets are used mainly in kitchens and bathrooms.*

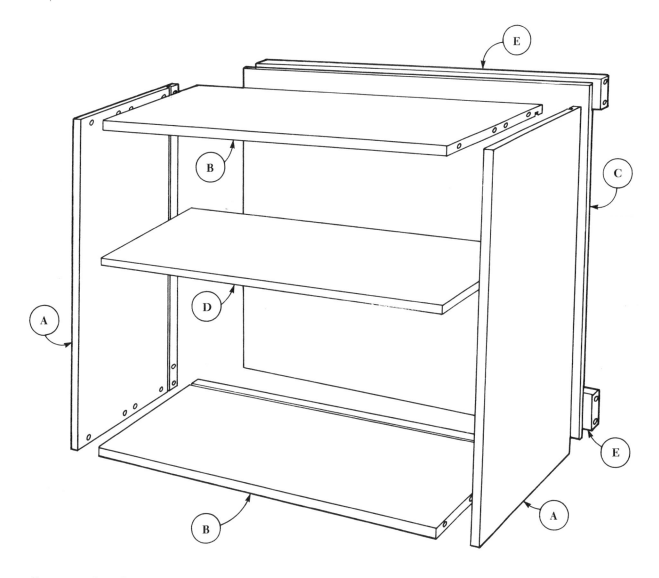

Illus. 7-2. *Plans for an overhead cabinet (exploded view). See the Bill of Materials on pages 112 and 113.*

Base Module

A base module is built to rest on the floor and to have a countertop attached to it (Illus. 7-5). A 4″ toe-kick (at the bottom of the base cabinet) is recessed back 3″. Make a cutout in the side of the cabinet to allow for the toe-kick.

Make the notch for the toe-kick, using a circular saw. You can't cut all the way to the corner without cutting past the line. Use a handsaw to complete the cut (Illus. 7-6). If you use a sabre saw to make the toe-kick cut, you can stop right at the corner.

An attaching cleat (behind the back at the top of the cabinet) attaches the cabinet to the wall.

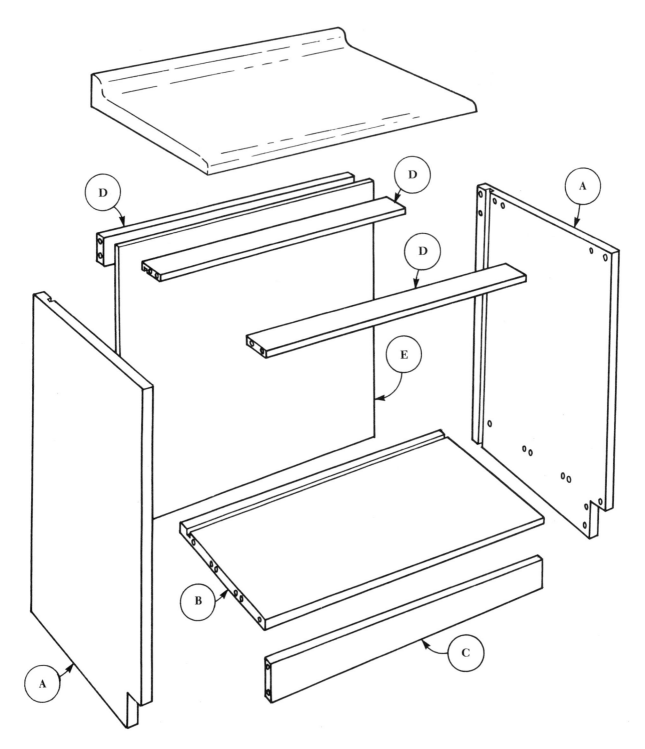

Illus. 7-3. *Plans for a base cabinet (exploded view).*
See the Bill of Materials on pages 114 and 115.

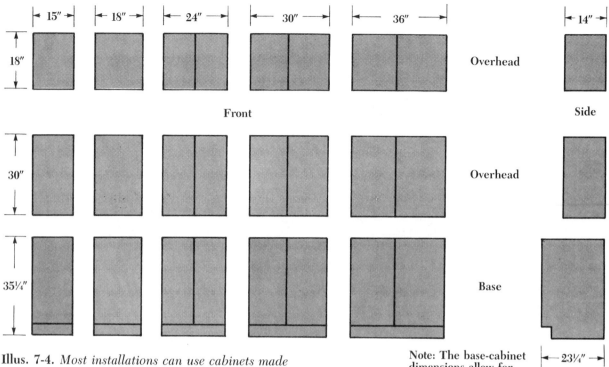

Illus. 7-4. *Most installations can use cabinets made to these standard sizes.*

Note: The base-cabinet dimensions allow for a countertop that's ¾″ thick, with a ¾″ front overhang.

The cleat is ¾″ thick and 4″ wide. To allow room for the cleat, the groove for the back is set back from the edge ¾″.

A solid top isn't necessary, since you'll install a countertop atop the base cabinet. Attach 4″-wide cleats at the front and back. Attach the countertop with screws driven up through these cleats.

Once you've built the carcass of the base cabinet, add doors or drawers, as needed. Illustrations 7-7 through 7-22 show the construction of a base cabinet.

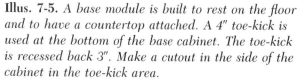

Illus. 7-5. *A base module is built to rest on the floor and to have a countertop attached. A 4″ toe-kick is used at the bottom of the base cabinet. The toe-kick is recessed back 3″. Make a cutout in the side of the cabinet in the toe-kick area.*

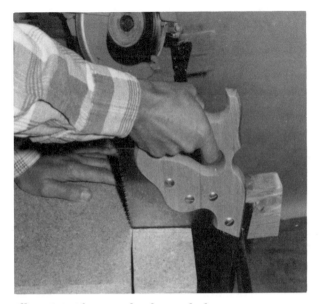

Illus. 7-6. *If you make the toe-kick cut using a circular saw, you'll need to use a handsaw to finish the cut at the corner.*

Illus. 7-7. *Lay out the parts on the sheet of particleboard. Position and clamp down the guide board, then cut out the parts using a portable circular saw.*

Illus. 7-8. *Cut a groove for the back in the bottom (Part B), the sides (Part A), and in one of the top cleats. The groove is ⅛" wide by ⅜" deep and set back from the edge ¾". The groove in the cleat will be easy to cut if you cut it first, before you cut out the cleat from a larger piece. This gives you enough room to clamp down the guide board.*

Illus. 7-9. *Lay out the dowel joints for the bottom shelf. The holes in the shelf should be 5/16" diameter and 1⅛" deep. Place one hole 16 mm in from the front and one hole 16 mm in from the groove at the back. Drill four more dowel holes between these first two. Space 160 mm from the front hole to the next one, then space 32 mm to the next hole. After that space 160 mm again and then 32 mm.*

Illus. 7-11. *Drill two holes in each end of the toe-kick board (Part C). The holes should be ⁵⁄₁₆″ in diameter by 1⅛″ deep and spaced 16 mm from each edge. Draw a line on the side indicating the back of the toe-kick. Use the same dowelling-jig setup as was described in the previous step. Place the toe-kick on the side and line up the notch in the dowelling jig with the line on the side. Clamp the toe-kick in place and position the dowelling jig on the first dowel. Drill the dowel hole, move to the next location, and then drill the other hole. Repeat the procedure on the other side.*

Illus. 7-10. *After you've drilled the holes in the shelf (Part B), draw a line on the side (Part A) indicating the bottom of the shelf. Remove the guide fence from the dowelling jig and set the depth stop to make a ½″-deep hole. Temporarily place dowels in the end of the shelf and lay the shelf on top of the side. Align the notch in the drill jig with the line and then clamp the shelf to the side.*

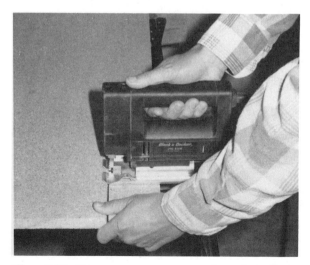

Illus. 7-12. *Now you can cut a notch in the side for the toe-kick (Part A). Don't cut the notch before you make the dowel joints for the bottom shelf and the toe-kick, because if you do, you won't have any place to clamp the dowelling jig in the front. You can use a circular saw and then finish the cut with a handsaw, or you could make the entire cut using a sabre saw, as shown here.*

Illus. 7-13. *Drill the dowel holes in the ends of the cleats (Part D). The holes are ⁵⁄₁₆″ diameter and 1⅛″ deep. The holes are spaced 16 mm in from each edge on all of the cleats, except the one that's grooved. The rear hole in the grooved cleat is 16 mm in from the groove.*

Illus. 7-14. *Temporarily place dowels in the cleats. Now clamp the cleat to the side, where it will serve as a guide for the dowelling jig as you drill the ½"-deep holes in the side. Be sure to line up the groove in the top rear cleat with the groove in the side.*

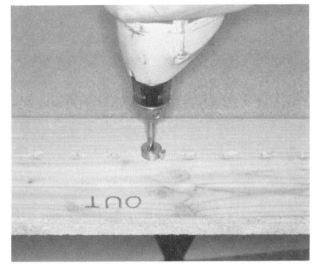

Illus. 7-15. *Use the 2 × 4 jig described in chapter 2 to drill the ¼" diameter by ½"-deep holes for the adjustable shelves.*

Illus. 7-16. *Apply glue to the joints and then assemble the parts. First attach the bottom shelf (Part B) to one of the sides (Part A).*

Illus. 7-17. *Now attach the toe-kick board (Part C) to the side.*

Overhead Cabinets

Overhead cabinets are similar to the one shown in chapter 2, except that the groove for the back

Illus. 7-18. *Put some glue in the groove and slip the back (Part E) into the grooves in the already-assembled side and bottom shelf.*

Illus. 7-19. *Now attach the cleats (Part D) to the side. Put some glue in the groove in the rear top cleat and align the back with the groove as you install the cleat.*

Illus. 7-20. *Finally, install the second side. Line up the dowels in the bottom shelf and the toe-kick first. Now work the back into the groove as you line up the cleats.*

Illus. 7-21. *Square up the cabinet, then clamp the joints using bar clamps. Leave the clamps in place for at least one hour.*

is set back ¾″, and attaching cleats are added at the top and bottom. The cleats are very important, since they support the weight of the cabinet when it's attached to the wall. Use two dowels at each end of the cleats to attach them to the sides of the cabinet.

An overhead cabinet for a laundry room or a storage room is a good project for novices, since construction is fairly simple. For detailed directions, refer to chapter 2. Illustrations 7-23 through 7-36 show the construction of overhead cabinets.

Illus. 7-22. *Build and install the drawers and the doors following the step-by-step directions found in chapters 3 and 4.*

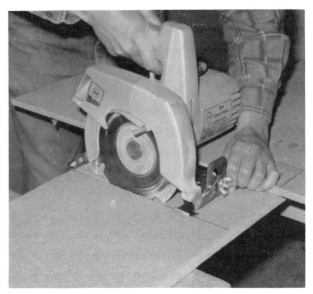

Illus. 7-23. *Lay out the parts on the sheet of particleboard. Position and clamp down the guide board, then cut out the parts using a portable circular saw. Make the long cuts first, then cut the parts to length.*

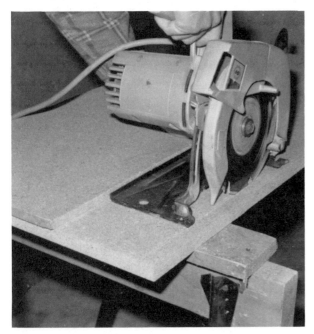

Illus. 7-24. *Cut a groove in the sides (Part A) (where the back will go), top and bottom (Part B). The groove is ⅛" wide by ⅜" deep and set back from the edge ¾". Use a board that's clamped to the parts to guide the circular saw.*

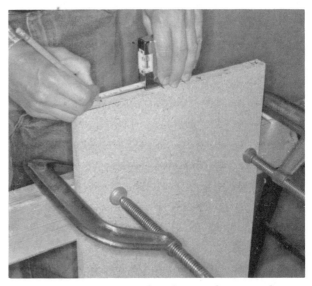

Illus. 7-25. *Lay out the dowel joints between the top and the bottom (Part B) and the sides (Part A). The holes in the top and bottom should be ⁵⁄₁₆" diameter and 1⅛" deep. Position one hole 16 mm in from the front and one hole 16 mm in from the groove at the back. Drill two more dowel holes between the first two. Space 112 mm from the front hole to the next one, then space 32 mm to the next hole.*

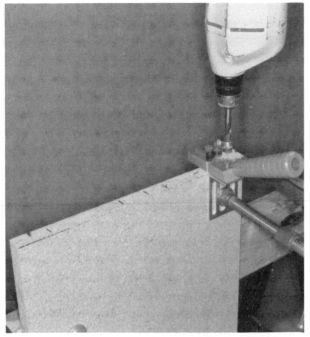

Illus. 7-26. *Drill the holes in the ends of Part B. Clamp the board to a sawhorse, then position the dowelling jig and clamp it in place. Drill the hole so that the depth stop is set to make a 1⅛"-deep hole.*

Illus. 7-27. *Temporarily place dowels in the ends of Part A. Lay Part A groove-side down on the saw-horses. Place Part B groove-side up, on top of Part A. Make sure that the joint numbers match, and then clamp the boards together. Place the slot in the dowelling jig guide fence over one of the dowels and clamp the jig in place. Drill the holes with the depth stop set to make a ½"-deep hole.*

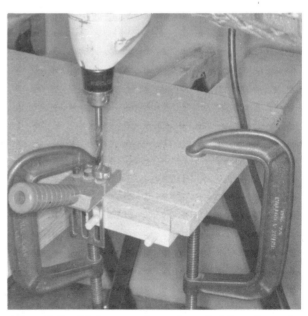

Illus. 7-28. *Drill the dowel holes in the ends of the cleats (Part E). The holes are 5/16" diameter and 1⅛" deep. The holes are spaced 16 mm in from each edge.*

Illus. 7-29. *Make a mark on the side ¾" in from the end. Temporarily place dowels in the cleats and then align the cleat with the mark. Clamp the cleat to the side to serve as a guide for the dowelling jig as you drill the ½"-deep holes in the side.*

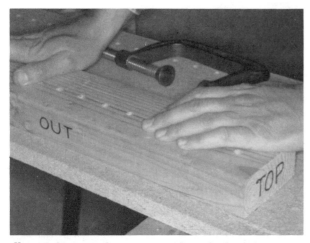

Illus. 7-30. *Use the 2 × 4 jig (described in chapter 2) to drill the ¼" diameter by ½"-deep holes for the adjustable shelves.*

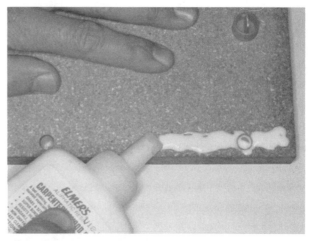

Illus. 7-31. *Apply glue to the joints and assemble the parts. Spread the glue around inside the dowel holes.*

Illus. 7-32. *First assemble the joint between one side (Part A) and the bottom (Part B).*

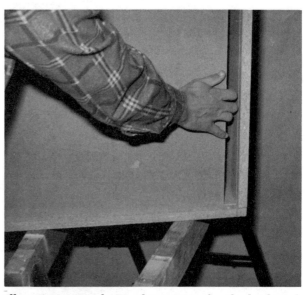

Illus. 7-33. *Put glue in the grooves for the back and then slide the back into the grooves in the two assembled parts.*

Installation

After you've built the cabinets, install them. Installation for this type of cabinet isn't too complex. The most important thing is to anchor the cabinets firmly to the wall by using 4"-long screws driven through the cleats and into the wall studs. Before starting the installation, find the stud locations in the walls, using an electronic stud finder (Illus. 7-37). The stud finder has bulbs that light up when the finder locates a stud. To locate the studs, put the stud finder against the wall, turn it on, and then rub it across the wall. When the bulbs light up, mark the stud location and then move on until you find the next

Illus. 7-34. *Attach the top (Part B), and then insert the cleats (Part E). After the cleats are in place, attach the second side.*

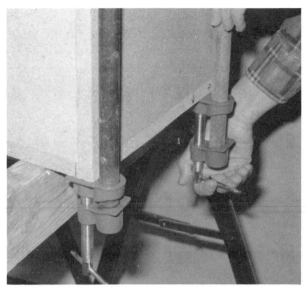

Illus. 7-35. *Square up the cabinet, then clamp the joints using bar clamps. Leave the clamps in place for at least one hour.*

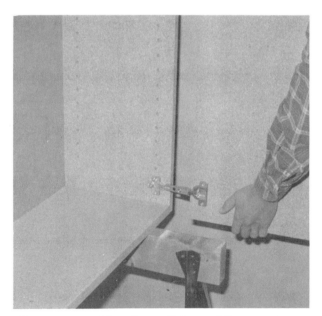

Illus. 7-36. *Build and install doors following the step-by-step directions found in chapter 3.*

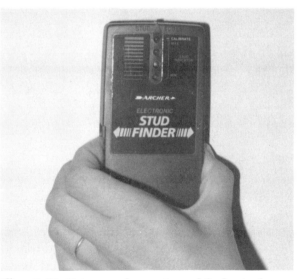

Illus. 7-37. *Using an electronic stud-finder is the easiest way to locate wall studs. Indicator lights flash at each stud location as the device is passed along the surface of the wall.*

stud. When you've located all of the studs, begin mounting the overhead cabinets.

Mark the location of the cabinet on the wall using a pencil. Use a level to make the lines level and plumb. A helpful trick when mounting overhead cabinets is to attach a board to the wall along the bottom line to help support the cabinet as you attach it. After the cabinets are in place, remove the board and fill in the screw holes that are left in the wall (Illus. 7-38).

Since the entire weight of the overhead cabinet (and its contents) is supported by the screws

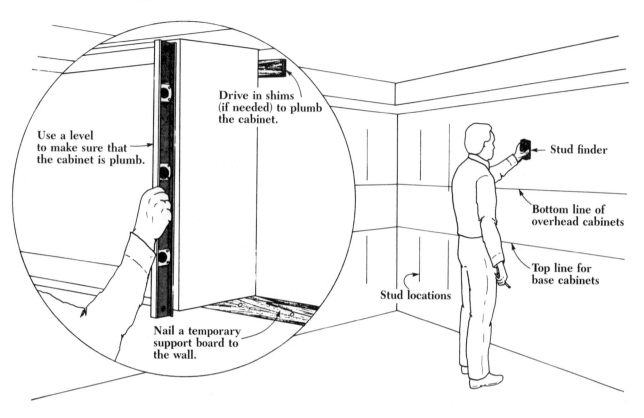

Illus. 7-38. *Draw lines on the wall to indicate the cabinet locations. Make sure the lines are level and plumb by using a level as you draw them. A board attached to the wall along the bottom line of the overhead cabinets will help to align and support the cabinets as you attach them to the wall. Use an electronic stud finder to locate the studs, and then mark their location on the wall.*

that attach it to the wall, it's very important that the cabinet be attached to the wall studs. Use a tape measure to transfer the stud locations from the wall to the cabinet. Drill screw holes through the back of the cabinet. At each stud location, drill two holes in the top cleat and one in the bottom cleat.

To lessen the weight of the cabinet before you lift it into place, remove the doors and shelves; then lift it into place. This is a two-person job.

While one person holds the cabinet in place, the other should quickly drive two screws through the upper attaching cleat and into the wall studs (Illus. 7-39). This should hold the weight of the cabinet as you add more screws. Put two 4″-long screws through the top cleat into every stud that falls within the inside dimensions

of the cabinet. One screw into each stud is all that's needed along the bottom cleat.

If you install more than one cabinet, place the next one against the side of the first and then clamp the two together. Drive screws through the side of one cabinet into the side of the other, then attach the second cabinet to the wall. If the wall isn't smooth, you may need to put shims (thin strips of wood or hardboard) between the wall and the back of the cabinet. After the cabinet is attached to the wall, reinstall the shelves and the doors.

To install the base cabinets, put them in position and make sure that they're level and that they line up with each other. You may need to shim under some of the cabinets to compensate for unevenness in the floor. You can buy wedge-

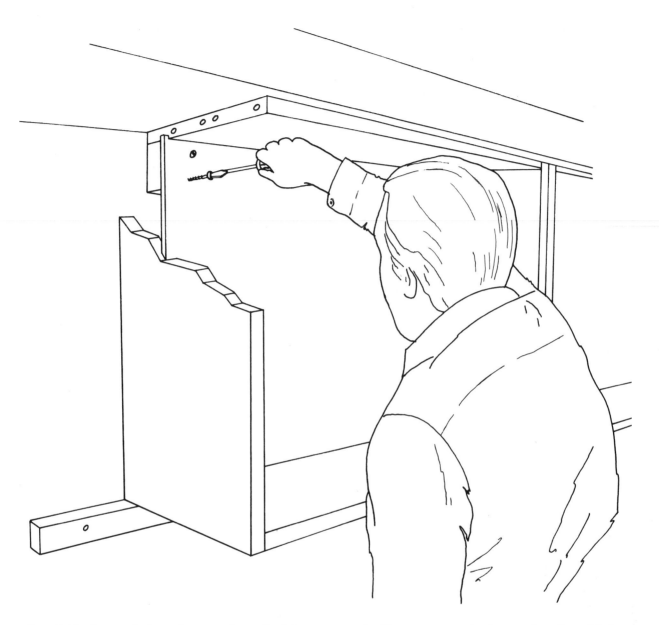

Illus. 7-39. *To attach the cabinet to the wall, drive screws through the cleat in the cabinet into the wall studs. Use two screws in the top cleat for added support.*

shaped shims just for this purpose. If the gap is large, you may be able to use a piece of hardboard as a shim (Illus. 7-40).

Clamp side-by-side cabinets together and drive screws through the side of one into the side of the other.

Drive screws through the back and the attaching cleat into the wall. For the best results, find the wall studs using an electronic stud finder, and then attach the cabinet to the stud, using long screws.

After the cabinets are firmly attached to the wall, put the countertop in place. A ready-made countertop called a "post-formed" plastic-laminate counter can be used with this type of cabinet. A post-formed countertop is easy for a

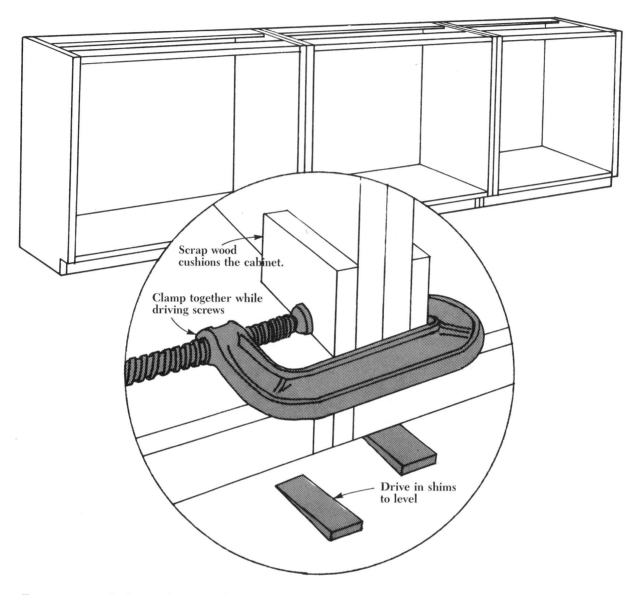

Illus. 7-40. *Put the base cabinets in their proper location and clamp them together. Check them to be sure they're level. Make necessary adjustments by putting shims between the cabinet and the floor.*

novice to install. Apply some construction adhesive (using a caulking gun) to the top cleats on the cabinets. Lay the countertop in place and drive a few screws up through the cleat and into the bottom of the countertop. Be sure to use screws that won't break through the surface of the countertop. After the countertop is anchored in place, attach the end cap (it comes with the countertop) to hide the rough ends (Illus. 7-41).

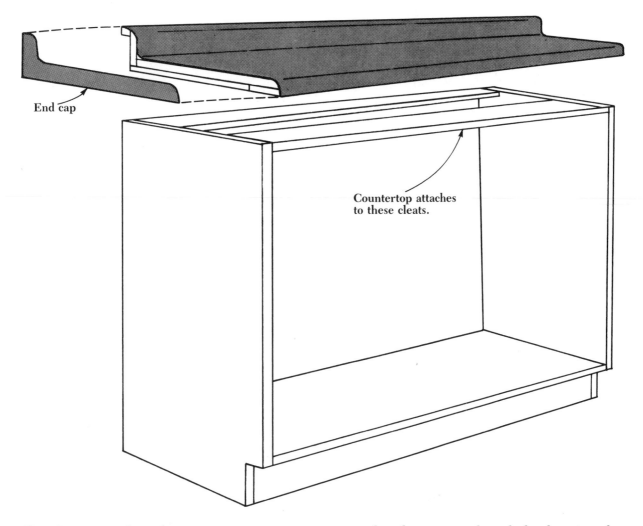

End cap

Countertop attaches to these cleats.

Illus. 7-41. *A post-formed countertop is easy to install. Apply construction adhesive to the top cleats on the cabinet. Place the counter on top of the cabinets, then drive screws through the cleats into the bottom of the counter. An end-cap kit is used to hide the exposed ends of the countertop.*

Bill of Materials

The following lists give the sizes for each part of the cabinet modules shown in Illus. 7-4. The letters refer to the labels on Illustrations 7-2 and 7-3. All dimensions are actual, in inches.

CABINET TYPE: OVERHEAD
SIZE: 18″ high × 15″ wide × 14″ deep
REFER TO ILLUS. 7-2

PART	DESCRIPTION	SIZE	NO. REQ'D
A	sides	¾ × 18 × 13¼	2
B	top & bottom	¾ × 13½ × 13¼	2
C	back	⅛ × 17¼ × 14¼	1
D	shelf	¾ × 13⅜ × 12⅜	varies
E	cleats	¾ × 4 × 13½	2
F	door	¾ × 15 × 18	1

SIZE: 18″ high × 18″ wide × 14″ deep

PART	DESCRIPTION	SIZE	NO. REQ'D
A	sides	¾ × 18 × 13¼	2
B	top & bottom	¾ × 16½ × 13¼	2
C	back	⅛ × 17¼ × 17¼	1
D	shelf	¾ × 16⅜ × 12⅜	varies
E	cleats	¾ × 4 × 16½	2
F	door	¾ × 18 × 18	1

SIZE: 18″ high × 24″ wide × 14″ deep

PART	DESCRIPTION	SIZE	NO. REQ'D
A	sides	¾ × 18 × 13¼	2
B	top & bottom	¾ × 22½ × 13¼	2
C	back	⅛ × 17¼ × 23¼	1
D	shelf	¾ × 22⅜ × 12⅜	varies
E	cleats	¾ × 4 × 22½	2
F	doors	¾ × 12 × 18	2

SIZE: 18″ high × 30″ wide × 14″ deep

PART	DESCRIPTION	SIZE	NO. REQ'D
A	sides	¾ × 18 × 13¼	2
B	top & bottom	¾ × 28½ × 13¼	2
C	back	⅛ × 17¼ × 29¼	1
D	shelf	¾ × 28⅜ × 12⅜	varies
E	cleats	¾ × 4 × 28½	2
F	door	¾ × 15 × 18	1

SIZE: 18″ high × 36″ wide × 14″ deep

PART	DESCRIPTION	SIZE	NO. REQ'D
A	sides	¾ × 18 × 13¼	2
B	top & bottom	¾ × 34½ × 13¼	2
C	back	⅛ × 17¼ × 35¼	1
D	shelf	¾ × 34⅜ × 12⅜	varies
E	cleats	¾ × 4 × 13½	2
F	door	¾ × 18 × 18	1

SIZE: 30″ high × 15″ wide × 14″ deep

PART	DESCRIPTION	SIZE	NO. REQ'D
A	sides	¾ × 30 × 13¼	2
B	top & bottom	¾ × 13½ × 13¼	2
C	back	⅛ × 29¼ × 14¼	1
D	shelf	¾ × 13⅜ × 12⅜	varies
E	cleats	¾ × 4 × 13½	2
F	door	¾ × 15 × 30	1

SIZE: 30″ high × 18″ wide × 14″ deep

PART	DESCRIPTION	SIZE	NO. REQ'D
A	sides	¾ × 30 × 13¼	2
B	top & bottom	¾ × 16½ × 13¼	2
C	back	⅛ × 29¼ × 17¼	1
D	shelf	¾ × 16⅜ × 12⅜	varies
E	cleats	¾ × 4 × 16½	2
F	door	¾ × 18 × 30	1

SIZE: 30″ high × 24″ wide × 14″ deep

PART	DESCRIPTION	SIZE	NO. REQ'D
A	sides	¾ × 30 × 13¼	2
B	top & bottom	¾ × 22½ × 13¼	2
C	back	⅛ × 29¼ × 23¼	1
D	shelf	¾ × 22⅜ × 12⅜	varies
E	cleats	¾ × 4 × 22½	2
F	door	¾ × 12 × 30	2

SIZE: 30″ high × 30″ wide × 14″ deep

PART	DESCRIPTION	SIZE	NO. REQ'D
A	sides	¾ × 30 × 13¼	2
B	top & bottom	¾ × 28½ × 13¼	2
C	back	⅛ × 29¼ × 29¼	1
D	shelf	¾ × 28⅜ × 12⅜	varies
E	cleats	¾ × 4 × 28½	2
F	door	¾ × 15 × 30	1

	SIZE: 30″ high × 36″ wide × 14″ deep		
PART	**DESCRIPTION**	**SIZE**	**NO. REQ'D**
A	sides	¾ × 30 × 13¼	2
B	top & bottom	¾ × 34½ × 13¼	2
C	back	⅛ × 29¼ × 35¼	1
D	shelf	¾ × 34⅜ × 12⅜	varies
E	cleats	¾ × 4 × 13½	2
F	door	¾ × 18 × 30	1

CABINET TYPE: BASE
SIZE: 36″ high × 15″ wide × 24″ deep
REFER TO ILLUS. 7-3

PART	**DESCRIPTION**	**SIZE**	**NO. REQ'D**
A	sides	¾ × 35¼ × 23¼	2
B	bottom	¾ × 13½ × 23¼	1
C	toe-kick	¾ × 13½ × 4	1
D	cleats	¾ × 13½ × 4	3
E	back	⅛ × 14¼ × 30½	1
F	door	¾ × 31¼ × 15	1
G	shelf	¾ × 13⅜ × 22⅜	varies

	SIZE: 36″ high × 18″ wide × 24″ deep		
PART	**DESCRIPTION**	**SIZE**	**NO. REQ'D**
A	sides	¾ × 35¼ × 23¼	2
B	bottom	¾ × 16½ × 23¼	1
C	toe-kick	¾ × 16½ × 4	1
D	cleats	¾ × 16½ × 4	3
E	back	⅛ × 17¼ × 30½	1
F	door	¾ × 31¼ × 18	1
G	shelf	¾ × 16⅜ × 22⅜	varies

	SIZE: 36″ high × 24″ wide × 24″ deep		
PART	**DESCRIPTION**	**SIZE**	**NO. REQ'D**
A	sides	¾ × 35¼ × 23¼	2
B	bottom	¾ × 22½ × 23¼	1
C	toe-kick	¾ × 22½ × 4	1
D	cleats	¾ × 22½ × 4	3
E	back	⅛ × 23¼ × 30½	1
F	door	¾ × 31¼ × 12	2
G	shelf	¾ × 22⅜ × 22⅜	varies

SIZE: 36″ high × 30″ wide × 24″ deep			
PART	**DESCRIPTION**	**SIZE**	**NO. REQ'D**
A	sides	¾ × 35¼ × 23¼	2
B	bottom	¾ × 28½ × 23¼	1
C	toe-kick	¾ × 28½ × 4	1
D	cleats	¾ × 28½ × 4	3
E	back	⅛ × 29¼ × 30½	1
F	doors	¾ × 31¼ × 15	2
G	shelf	¾ × 28⅜ × 22⅜	varies

SIZE: 36″ high × 36″ wide × 24″ deep			
PART	**DESCRIPTION**	**SIZE**	**NO. REQ'D**
A	sides	¾ × 35¼ × 23¼	2
B	bottom	¾ × 34½ × 23¼	1
C	toe-kick	¾ × 34½ × 4	1
D	cleats	¾ × 34½ × 4	3
E	back	⅛ × 35¼ × 30½	1
F	doors	¾ × 31¼ × 18	2
G	shelf	¾ × 34⅜ × 22⅜	varies

Chapter 8
PLASTIC LAMINATES

Plastic laminates can be used to cover part of, or all of a cabinet. They are particularly useful for kitchen cabinets that receive heavy use and that need constant cleaning (Illus. 8-1). Plastic laminate is more durable, water-resistant and is easier to clean than a painted surface is. Any of the cabinets described in this book can be covered with plastic laminate. Built-in cabinets are frequently covered with plastic laminate, but plastic laminate can also be used on freestanding cabinets (Illus. 8-2). Cabinets that will be covered with plastic laminate should be made from particleboard or plywood. Solid lumber is not a good substrate material, because it expands and contracts with changes in humidity. These dimensional changes can cause cracks in the plastic laminate, or open joints, or poor bonding. Particleboard is an ideal substrate. Most professionally built cabinets that are covered with plastic laminate are made from particleboard. If you use plywood, avoid using fir plywood with a

very prominent grain. The grain can "telegraph" through the plastic laminate and show on the surface; also, the variation between the hard and the soft portions of the grain can lead to poor adhesion.

Technically speaking, the name of this material is high-pressure decorative plastic laminate. "High-pressure" refers to the manufacturing process that forms the laminate. High-pressure laminate is a tough material that can withstand some abrasion and temperatures up to 275°F (135°C). Plastic laminate is available in a wide range of colors and patterns (Illus. 8-3). The wood-grain patterns are particularly useful in cabinetmaking. Some laminates are available with metallic surface finishes, such as brass and aluminum. Laminates have several surface finishes available. The two most common finishes are gloss and satin. Gloss is smooth, highly reflective, and it intensifies the color. Gloss is harder to care for than other finishes because

Illus. 8-1. *Plastic laminate, an ideal covering for kitchen cabinets, is durable and water-resistant. Frameless cabinets are easy to cover with plastic laminate because there are no face frames to cover.*

Illus. 8-2. *This small cabinet is covered with a glossy black plastic laminate. This laminate looks like an oriental lacquered finish, but it's much more durable.*

Illus. 8-3. *Plastic laminate is available in many patterns and finishes. Laminate dealers will have several sets of samples like this. You can turn a simple particleboard cabinet into something really impressive by covering it with laminates in one of many wood grain patterns, or a solid color, or even a metallic finish.*

it shows finger smudges and minor scratches. Satin, a semigloss finish, is easier to maintain than gloss because it hides finger marks and small scratches. A textured finish is often used with wood-grain patterns. Textured finish is easy to care for (like the satin finish), and it makes the wood-grain pattern look more realistic. A heavily embossed surface ("three-dimensional") is used to simulate leather or slate or to imitate caning or a coarse fabric. Because of the deep surface crevasses, it's difficult to clean, but it hides finger smudges and small scratches very well. There are two thicknesses of plastic laminate. The most widely used thickness (1/16″) can be used for most applications. When the surface doesn't need to be particularly durable, 1/32″-thick plastic laminate can be used.

Many home supply centers and lumberyards sell plastic laminate in precut sizes. If you cover a large cabinet, it makes sense to buy full sheets from a wholesaler. You'll save money this way. Standard sheet sizes are: 4′ × 8′, 4′ × 10′ and 4′ × 12′. Plastic laminate is brittle. Be careful when you handle it before it's bonded to the cabinet. The best way to transport full sheets of plastic laminate is to roll them up first. The roll should have a diameter of 18″ or more. If you roll it tighter, you may crack the laminate. When you buy full sheets of laminate, the salespeople will usually roll it up for you and secure it using a cardboard band (Illus. 8-4). If you roll it yourself, secure it with twine. Place a piece of cardboard between the twine and the edge of the plastic laminate. Without the cardboard, the twine itself can crack the edge (Illus. 8-5). Keep the laminate rolled until you're ready to use it, then unroll it carefully. Don't let the roll spring open, because you'll damage the plastic laminate. Hold the edges and slowly unroll it. Examine the laminate for damage. If there's a crack, cover it with some

Illus. 8-4. *When you buy full sheets of plastic laminate, the dealer will roll them up like this. Plastic laminate is brittle and it will crack if handled improperly. Rolling up the sheets like this protects them during transport.*

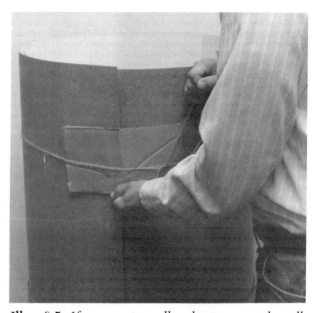

Illus. 8-5. *If you must reroll a sheet, secure the roll with twine, but be sure to place a piece of cardboard over the edge of the sheet, as shown here. If you don't use the cardboard, the twine will crack the edge of the plastic laminate.*

strong packing tape. This will keep the crack from spreading (Illus. 8-6). Plan your cuts so that the crack falls in a waste area.

overhang will be trimmed off later, after the plastic laminate is bonded to the substrate.

Because plastic laminate is brittle and thin, use fine-tooth saw blades. Always wear eye protection when you cut plastic laminate, since

Cutting Plastic Laminates

Plastic laminate can be cut using any of several tools: table saws, portable circular saws, sabre saws, tin snips, or special carbide-tipped scoring tools. Always cut the plastic laminate oversize. You usually want ¼" overhang, so add ½" to both the length and the width of the laminate. The

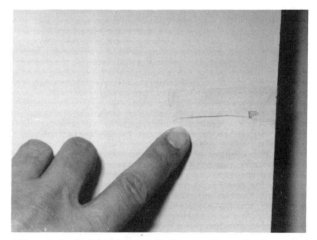

Illus. 8-6. *If you should find a crack in the laminate, cover it with packing tape on both sides of the sheet. The tape will keep the crack from spreading. If the crack is small, you can usually plan your cuts so that the crack will fall in the waste area.*

Illus. 8-7. *If you use a table saw to cut the laminate, here's a trick to help you control the sheet as you cut. Bend the outside edge, as shown here. This keeps the sheet rigid and flat against the table. Have someone hold the back of the sheet as it comes out of the table saw.*

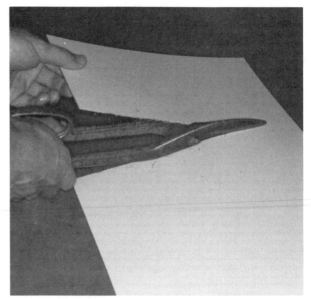

Illus. 8-8. *You could use tin snips to cut plastic laminate, but they leave a rougher cut than other tools do, so leave a little more overhang to be sure that all of the rough edge will be trimmed away.*

small sharp chips tend to fly out of the cut. I prefer to wear a full face shield when cutting laminate. A sabre saw is easy for a beginner to handle. Use a fine-toothed metal cutting blade. Take your time and don't force the cut. If you have a table saw, you can also use it for cutting plastic laminate. A table saw is particularly useful for cutting the narrow strips used to cover the edges. When you cut from a full sheet of laminate

you'll need plenty of room. Move the saw outside, if necessary. Because it's so flexible, plastic laminate is difficult to handle on the table saw. If you bend the laminate along the direction of the cut, it will be more rigid and easier to handle on the saw (Illus. 8-7). Set the rip fence to the width needed. If there is a small gap between the bottom of the fence and the table, the plastic laminate can get under the fence and jam. To avoid

Illus. 8-9. *Scoring tools are easy to use and they're less expensive than some of the other tools used to cut and trim plastic laminate. The carbide-tipped scoring knife in the middle is used to cut pieces of laminate to rough size. The trimmer on the right trims the laminate to the exact size after it's been bonded to the cabinet. The beveller on the left is used to smooth the edge after trimming and to give the edge a slight bevel. The bevel makes the edge more durable.*

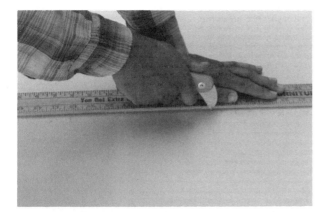

Illus. 8-10. *Use a straightedge to guide the scoring knife. For most cuts, use a yardstick. When the cut is too long even for a yardstick, use a longer board with a straight edge. Clamp the straightedge in place to keep it from slipping out of position as you make the cut. A couple of small spring clamps are good for this, but you could use C clamps, as well. Put a board under the cut and then clamp the board, the laminate and the straightedge together.*

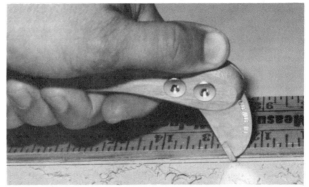

Illus. 8-11. *Use moderate pressure on the scoring knife as you make the first pass, then press harder on the knife as you make a second pass. Make additional passes to deepen the cut until the cut is about halfway through the laminate. This photo shows how to hold the knife at the best cutting angle. When the knife cuts properly, it produces small shavings like the ones shown here. If the knife isn't cutting smoothly, raise or lower the handle slightly until you get a smooth cut.*

this, clamp a board to the fence and make sure that the bottom edge of the board is flush with the table.

Tin snips can also be used to cut plastic laminate (Illus. 8-8). The snips leave a rough edge and some small cracks. Leave a little more overhang than usual, so that all of the cracks will be trimmed off after the piece is bonded to the cabinet.

Carbide-tipped scoring tools can be used to cut plastic laminate (Illus. 8-9). This is one of the best methods for a beginner to use, because it's easy and it produces a clean edge. Since the sheet of plastic laminate can be laid on the floor, it's easy to cut from a full sheet. Mark the cutting line on the face of the plastic laminate, then place a straightedge (a yardstick or a board) along the line. A couple of small spring clamps can be used to hold the straightedge in place (Illus. 8-10). Pull the scoring knife along the line, using the straightedge as a guide. Make several passes until you've cut about halfway through the plastic laminate (Illus. 8-11). Break the piece along the scored line. Press down on the straightedge positioned along the line, and then lift up on the other piece. The plastic laminate will snap along

the line, making a clean break (Illus. 8-12). When you cut the narrow strips used to cover the edges, here's a helpful hint. Plastic laminate has

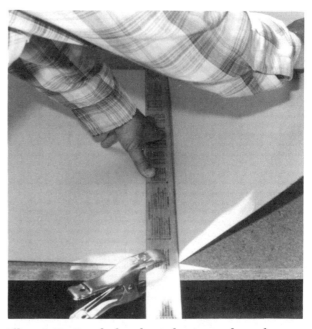

Illus. 8-12. *Break the plastic laminate along the scored line. Press down on the straightedge and lift the free end of the laminate until the laminate snaps along the scored line.*

a grain that runs in the same direction as the scratches on the back of the sheet. It's easy to break off narrow strips that run with the grain. You can break off a narrow strip across the grain, but it's likely that the strip will break in two.

Bonding

After the plastic laminate has been cut to the rough size, you'll be ready to bond it to the cabinet. Contact cement is the adhesive most often used. Be sure to use a new type of nonflammable contact cement that doesn't emit toxic fumes.

There are still a few cements available that may be flammable or toxic, so read the labels. Follow the label directions carefully. The directions given in this chapter are general for most types of contact cement, but drying times or other specifics may vary.

Follow a specific order to apply pieces of plastic laminate to a cabinet. Following this sequence will facilitate trimming and give better looking results, since the dark edge of the plastic laminate will not be so noticeable. There are several ways to cover the edges of a board. The method described here is called a "self-edge," because the same plastic laminate that covers the face of the board is used to cover the edge.

Illus. 8-13. *Apply plastic laminate to a cabinet door in the order shown here. Doors always require a backer to keep them from warping.*

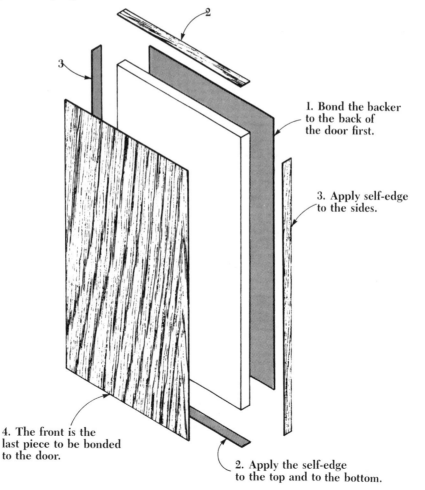

1. Bond the backer to the back of the door first.

3. Apply self-edge to the sides.

4. The front is the last piece to be bonded to the door.

2. Apply the self-edge to the top and to the bottom.

The first example is a cabinet door. On built-in cabinets, the doors and the drawer fronts may be the only parts of the cabinet that are covered with plastic laminate. A door needs laminate on both the front and the back, and on all the edges. The piece on the back is called a "balance sheet" or a "backer." The backer is used to balance the effects caused by applying plastic laminate to the front of the door. If you don't cover the back of the door with plastic laminate, the door will eventually warp. The backer keeps the door in balance and prevents warping. The backer must be the same thickness as the piece of laminate on the front, but it doesn't have to be the same pattern or color. Drawer fronts usually don't require a backer because these fronts are small and firmly attached to the drawer sides.

First bond the backer sheet to the back of the door, then trim to the edges (as described later). Next apply the strips to the top and to the bottom, and trim these strips, then apply them to the sides. After the side pieces are trimmed, bond the piece to the front (Illus. 8-13).

Illus. 8-14. *Follow this sequence when applying plastic laminate to the outside of a cabinet. You could reverse the order of steps 4 and 5. If you apply the top and bottom self-edge before the sides, you won't need to be as accurate when cutting the strips to length. Be sure to make the top and the bottom strips slightly shorter than necessary, never longer.*

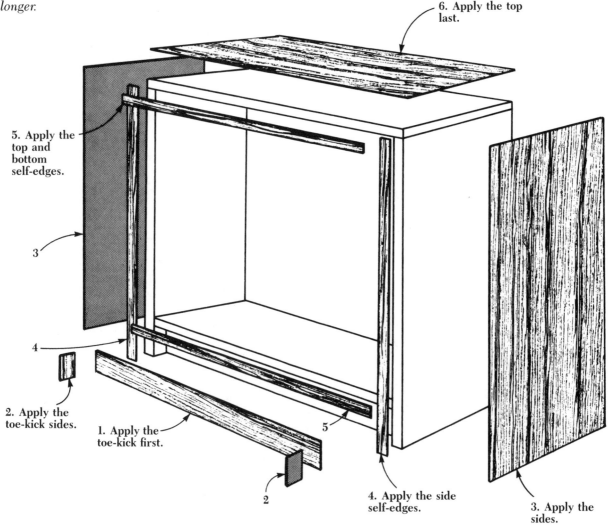

6. Apply the top last.

5. Apply the top and bottom self-edges.

3

4

2. Apply the toe-kick sides.

1. Apply the toe-kick first.

2

5

4. Apply the side self-edges.

3. Apply the sides.

The next example is a simple freestanding cabinet. You can apply plastic laminate just to the outside or to both the outside and the inside of the cabinet. The sides, the top and the bottom of a cabinet don't need backer sheets (like a door does) because the structure of the cabinet prevents these pieces from warping. Shelves *do* need balance sheets, so cover both sides of a shelf. Unless it's necessary for appearance, it's usually better *not* to apply laminate to the inside of a cabinet—it makes the process a lot more complicated. If you're using adjustable shelves, apply the plastic laminate *before* you drill the holes for the shelf support clips. If you *do* choose to cover the inside of the cabinet, all of the laminate should be applied to the inside of the cabinet before you apply any to the outside.

Cover the outside of a cabinet, beginning with the toe-kick. The procedure is more difficult if you haven't notched the sides of the cabinet in the toe-kick area, because you must trim the plastic laminate to the exact length before bonding it to the cabinet. If the sides are notched for the toe-kick, you can let the laminate overhang the edges and trim it after it's been applied. Trim the bottom edge of the laminate on the toe-kick after it's been bonded in place. If the sides are notched, then next apply the small piece of laminate to the sides in the toe-kick area. After the toe-kick area has been covered with laminate, apply the laminate to the sides of the cabinet.

Trim the sides and apply the front edging to the sides. Align the edging so that the edge is flush with the inside edge of the cabinet, leaving all of the overhang on the outside. This will make trimming easier and produces a better-looking joint between the side edging and the strips on the top and the bottom. Now cut the top and bottom edging strips to the exact length to fit between the side strips. Apply the top and bottom edging strips with the edge flush with the inside of the cabinet. Trim these strips. The final step is to apply the top piece of plastic laminate. Let it overhang on all edges. Trim it after it's bonded to the cabinet (Illus. 8-14).

Now let's discuss the specifics of bonding plastic laminate to a substrate (the wood of the cabinet). Contact cement can be applied either with a brush, a roller or a spray gun. For the beginner, the roller is probably best. Pour a small amount of cement into a paint-roller pan. First use a small, short-napped paint roller to apply the cement to the back of the plastic laminate. Cement always seems to take longer to dry on the plastic laminate than it does on the substrate. By applying the cement to the laminate first, both surfaces will be dry at approximately the same time. When the back of the plastic laminate is coated, apply cement to the substrate. Apply an even coat and try to avoid lumps or thick areas. Once you have a good coat, don't roll over the area again (Illus. 8-15). Let the cement dry, following the directions on the can, usually about 30 minutes. Follow the directions if a second coat is recommended. To see if the cement is dry, press your finger into the cement. If you can pull your finger away without some of the cement pulling off the board, then the cement is ready to bond.

Position carefully when you work with contact cement. Once the two surfaces touch, they will immediately stick together. If the pieces are out of position when this happens, you're in trouble. When the pieces are small, you can usually position them without too much trouble. Leave about ¼″ overhang on all sides, and press the piece against the substrate. Larger pieces re-

Illus. 8-15. *A small paint roller is an efficient way to spread the contact cement evenly. After you get an even coat, don't reroll over the same area—you may lift off some of the cement and weaken the bond.*

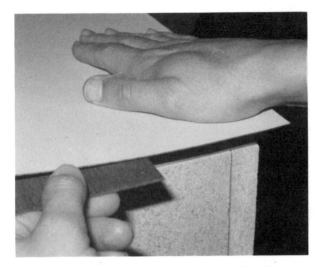

Illus. 8-16. *When the glue is dry, place the slip sheet on top of the cabinet and then place the plastic laminate on top of the slip sheet. Move the laminate into position with an equal overhang on all sides. Pull out the slip sheet a few inches and then press down on the laminate. The contact cement will grab as soon as the two surfaces are in contact. Now slide the slip sheet out some more, and press down another section of laminate. Repeat the procedure until the slip sheet is completely removed.*

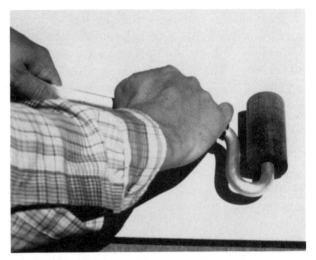

Illus. 8-17. *For contact cement to bond well, apply pressure evenly to the entire surface. A "J" roller can be used to apply the necessary pressure. Press down with your body weight and roll across the entire surface.*

quire a different technique. Use a "slip sheet" to keep the two surfaces from touching as you position the plastic laminate. The slip sheet (a piece of thin material that's placed in between the substrate and the plastic laminate) should be slightly larger than the substrate. Another piece of plastic laminate is a very good slip sheet. Making sure that there's no glue on the slip sheet, place it on top of the substrate. Now place the piece of plastic laminate on top of the slip sheet. Adjust the position of the plastic laminate so that there's a uniform overhang on all edges. Hold the plastic laminate in position and pull out the slip sheet about 2″ from one end. Press down on the plastic laminate in the area that's been exposed, bonding it to the substrate, then pull out some more of the slip sheet and press down on the next section. Continue in this manner until the slip sheet is completely removed (Illus. 8-16).

Once the plastic laminate is in place, it must be pressed firmly against the substrate. If you neglect this step, the bond will be poor and may

come apart. Professionals use "J" rollers to press the plastic laminate against the substrate. Press your body weight against the roller and roll evenly across the entire surface (Illus. 8-17). If you'll be doing a lot of plastic-laminate work, a "J" roller is a good investment. If you don't have this roller, place a small block of wood on the surface of the plastic laminate and pound on the block with a hammer. As you pound, move the block, so that the entire surface is uniformly pounded against the substrate.

Trimming

Each piece of plastic laminate is cut oversize and when it's applied, it overhangs the substrate. This overhang must be trimmed off before the next piece of laminate is applied. A router is one of the best tools to use to trim plastic laminate. A special trimming bit is needed to perform this operation. The trimming bit has a pilot that rides against the substrate and guides the router (Illus. 8-18). The bit will follow any irregularities in the edge of the substrate, so be sure that the edges are smooth.

Illus. 8-18. *After the plastic laminate is bonded to the surface, a router equipped with a laminate-trimming bit is one of the best tools for trimming away the overhang. The bit has a pilot that follows the edge of the cabinet and guides the router to cut the laminate flush with the edge. The bit shown here has a solid pilot. This is an inexpensive bit, and it will serve well for most do-it-yourself work. If you'll be doing a lot of work with plastic laminate, get a professional-type bit that has a ball-bearing pilot.*

Always wear eye protection when you trim with a router. A full face shield is best, because sharp chips may hit you in the face. Doors and drawers should be clamped to a bench or saw-horse for routing. Place the router base on the face of the plastic laminate and position the bit so that it doesn't quite touch the plastic laminate. Start the router and move the bit into the over-hang while keeping the router base riding flat on the face. When the bit pilot touches the edges of the substrate, move the router along the edge at a steady pace, keeping the pilot against the edge and the router base flat on the face. If glue builds up on the pilot, stop the router and unplug it, then scrape the glue off the bit. Built-up glue on the pilot can cause the bit to ride too far from the edge, leaving a slight overhang on the plastic laminate. If this happens, make a second pass

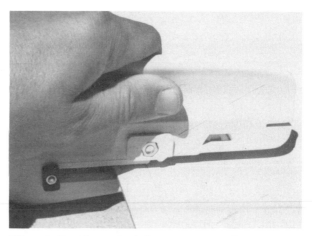

Illus. 8-19. *If you don't have a router, the scoring edge-trimmer can be used to trim the plastic laminate to size. A pilot on the trimmer rides against the edge of the board, guiding the blade that scores a line on the top face of the laminate. Make the first pass using light pressure, making sure that the pilot is following the edge. Press down harder on the next pass; the scored line will help to guide the cutter this time. Keep going over the line until the cut is about halfway through the laminate.*

Illus. 8-20. *Use the notch in the end of the trimmer to bend up on the waste side of the scored line. Start near one end and bend up until the laminate snaps, then move further down the line and bend up again. Repeat this procedure all along the line until the entire strip of waste breaks free.*

after cleaning the bit. If the bit is sharp and clean, you may not need to do anything else to the edge. Sometimes it's necessary to clean up the edge slightly, using a fine file or a block plane.

If you don't have a router, you could use a scoring-edge trimmer. This trimmer is slower (but cheaper) than a router, but it works well for small projects. The scoring-edge trimmer works on the same principle as the scoring knife (described in the section about cutting to size). The trimmer has a pilot that rubs against the edge of the substrate. Place the trimmer on the overhang with the pilot against the edge of the substrate. Run the trimmer along the edge and score a line on the face of the plastic laminate. Make several passes until the cut is about halfway through the laminate (Illus. 8-19). Bend up the overhang until it snaps off. The trimmer has a slot in the end

that can be used to snap off the overhang (Illus. 8-20).

Exposed edges will be more durable if you bevel them slightly, using a fine file. Hold the file at a slight angle, drawing it across the edge. If you don't want to file, get a bevelling router bit, or even a hand scraper that will put a bevel on the edge. If there are some gaps in a visible joint, fill them with a special type of filler made for use with plastic laminates. This filler comes in a variety of colors. After the job is done, wash the plastic laminate, using a rag moistened with water and mild detergent. This removes a protective coating that's found on some plastic laminate, and it will also clean up any leftover glue or finger marks. If you can't get glue off the face using detergent and water, buy a special solvent that the manufacturer of the contact cement recommends.

GLOSSARY

Aliphatic Resin A type of glue generally used for wood joinery, also called "carpenter's glue."

Backer (Balance Sheet) A sheet of material used on the back of a door when the front is covered with sheathing (plastic laminate, e.g.). Sheathing a door in this manner prevents the core material from dimensionally distorting.

Base Cabinet A cabinet that rests on the floor, the bottom unit of a modular cabinet system.

Bevel Inclined, angled, or slanted edge; not at a 90° angle.

Boring Machine A tool that drills several holes at once.

Brad Thin wire nail, with a small barrel-shaped head.

Burlap A coarse, heavy fabric, woven of jute or hemp.

Carbide A hard metal used for saw teeth; more brittle and harder than steel.

Carcass The basic box of a cabinet; the basic frame.

Chamfer The surface resulting from cutting away the angle at the intersection of two faces of a piece of wood.

Cheesecloth A lightweight cotton gauze.

Depth Stop A collar mounted on a drill that stops the bit when it reaches a certain depth in the work.

Dowelling Jig A tool that positions holes in the edge of a board, for dowel placement.

European (Frameless) System A method of cabinetry construction that uses the cabinet's sides for support, rather than a frame.

Factory Edge The edge of a factory-milled board or panel, considered to be both straight and square due to the precision of the factory's cutting tools.

Filler A paintlike substance that evens out a rough wood surface by filling in the tiny pores on the wood's surface.

Freestanding Moveable; not attached; not supported.

Gingerbread A board with a fancy edge; any elaborate, fancy or lavish architectural ornament.

Hardboard A sheet material made from compressed wood fibres.

Hardwood Woods from broad-leaved trees, such as oak, mahogany or walnut. The term has no relation to the actual hardness of the wood. See **Softwood**.

Hutch A low cupboard with open shelves above.

Joint Any place where two edges come together on a wood piece.

Kerf The cut made by a saw blade.

Knot The base of a branch, apparent in sawn lumber. As a potential weak spot, a knot is generally considered a defect.

Latex Paint A paint made with water-soluble "synthetic rubber."

Mitre Cut A cut made at a 45° angle. Two pieces mitred at this angle form a 90° angle.

Overhead Cabinet A cabinet generally mounted on a wall, below a ceiling; common in kitchens and baths.

Particleboard A sheet material made from pressed wood chips or wood particles.

Plastic Laminate A material used to cover cabinets, made of pressure-bonded layers of plastic.

Plywood A sheet material made by gluing together thin layers of wood.

Relief Cut A straight cut in from the edge of a board, through the waste area.

Sawhorse A flat-topped trestle used singly or in pairs to support a workpiece.

Scoring Tool A tool with a sharp edge that's used to make V-shaped grooves in brittle materials such as plastic laminates. The materials break along the scored line when they're bent.

Shim A tapered piece of material used to fill in a space; used for support, levelling, and adjustment.

Slip Sheet A sheet of material used to separate two surfaces that have glue on them; meant to prevent these two surfaces from adhering to each other.

Softwood Wood from trees that bear needles rather than broad leaves. Pine and fir are commonly used softwoods.

Square To ensure that all corners of a workpiece form perfect right (90°) angles.

Stain A coloring agent that penetrates wood pores.

Stud One of the smaller uprights in wall framing to which the wall sheathing is attached.

Substrate The bottom or under layer of a clad surface or structure.

Tack Cloth A specially treated sticky cloth used to remove dust or sawdust from wood surfaces.

Toe-Kick The space below the bottom shelf on the outside of a base cabinet; usually recessed from the front.

Utility Knife A knife with a retractable razor-blade edge.

Veneer A thin layer of wood (generally good quality) that's applied to an inferior substrate material.

Wood Putty A compound that's used to fill nail holes.

Index